arcocolourcollection

architecture

New European Architecture

architecture

Author

Francisco Asensio Cerver

Publishing Director

Paco Asensio

Proofreading

Tobias Willett

Graphic Design

Mireia Casanovas Soley, Quim Serra Catafau

© Copyright

Arco Editorial, S. A.

ISBN: 84-8185-015-2 (complete collection)
84-8185-016-0 (New European Architecture)

New European Architecture

The current panorama of architecture presents us with a degree of complexity in which the specialist critic does not always manage to establish the clear, meaningful criteria that help to elucidate the complicated framework.

With this contribution we seek to do no more than reveal a given reality which consists of a group of projects which are, by and large, a compilation of the latest architectural constructions completed in Europe over the last three years. We have therefore not attempted to give personal opinions in a categorical manner but rather to reveal certain tendencies and analyse their characteristics in order to provide the public with easier access to them. The lack of a historical perspective has made it difficult to establish a precise selection of the projects, and it has had to be based on the proven quality of these architects.

We must also bear in mind that this appraisal is rooted in a definite moment in time (the passage from one decade to another) which is characterised by the exacerbation and defence of individualism. This attitude is consequently seen in the execution of works which often end up as the personalised, subjective expression of a heterogeneous group of leading architects who will just as soon establish the sort of clear, open and sincere dialogue with architecture which is the fruit of a great personality – thereby making it a purely human activity – as they will become isolated and detached figures who create works full of structural virtuosity, distant and unconcerned with the hotly debated relationship between architecture and the public.

In the analysis of the projects that we present here, the common theme is variety, the reflection of the multiplicity of tastes and tendencies of our time.

These results make up the contents of this work: projects produced both by those who have consolidated their reputation, with a long career already behind them, and by younger names who are defin-

ing the current state of European architecture in a no less convincing manner.

European architecture, in its present state, is characterised by pluralism, be it as a result of a crisis of values, be it as a result of an unjustified defence of individualism, of an urge to dominate or of an alarming drying up of the sources of inspiration.

New European Architecture

architecture

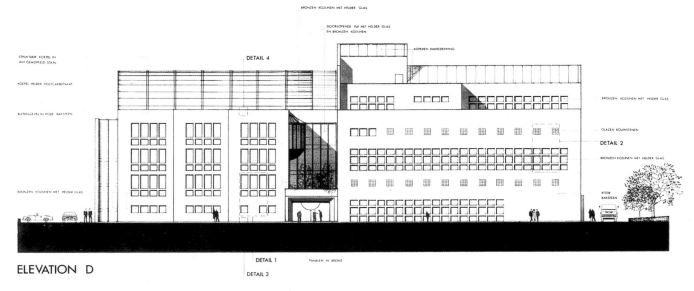

ELEVATION D

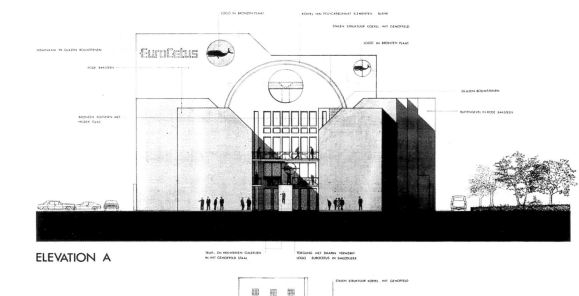

ELEVATION A

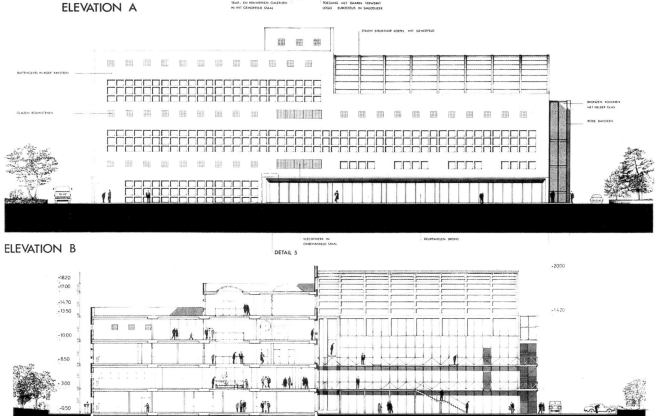

ELEVATION B

SECTION C·C

10

Eurocetus

Dante Benini & Ingex

The industrial building known as Eurocetus is located to the southeast of Amsterdam on the outskirts of the city. The 80 x 100 m site is surrounded by some very large buildings, such as the AMC (Academic Medical Center) and the IBM building, as well as smaller industrial and commercial constructions.

Born in Milan in 1947, Dante Benini began his professional training in Venice under Carlo Scarpa, continuing in England and later in Brazil where, in 1979, he received his degree in architecture from the Federal University of Brazil. In the same year, he founded Dante Benini & Ingex with offices in São Paulo and Milan. Milan has recently become the headquarters of his architectural practice. In addition to numerous industrial buildings and town planning projects, Benini has also designed houses,

offices, showrooms and shops in major cities and capitals all over the world. In 1986, his project for Farmitalia Carlo Erba was singled out by the Lombardy section of In-Arch (National Institute of Architecture). This led to an exhibition of Benini's work at the national In-Arch headquarters in Rome in 1988, and to the inclusion of twelve of his most interesting projects in a book published by Mondadori entitled Architetture e Progetti 1970-1987.

The Eurocetus building designed by Benini has a U-shaped layout, with two wings dominated by a central portion. This design stems from the search for the optimum layout to fulfill the needs of a research facility. The architect wanted a design in which the more flexible areas (office and service space) could be fitted in around the research area. The laboratories are located in the left

11

Partial view of the transparent roof.

Detail of the door on the front facade, showing the transparent roof.

Front facade.

Ground plan.

Plan of the first floor.

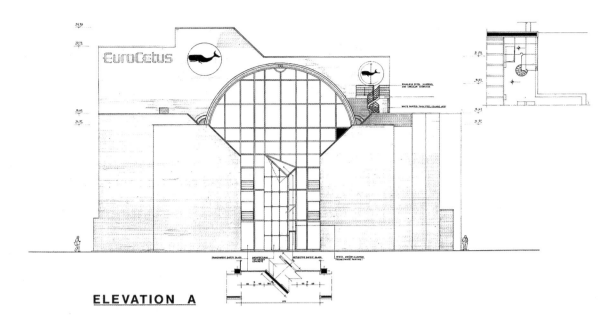

ELEVATION A

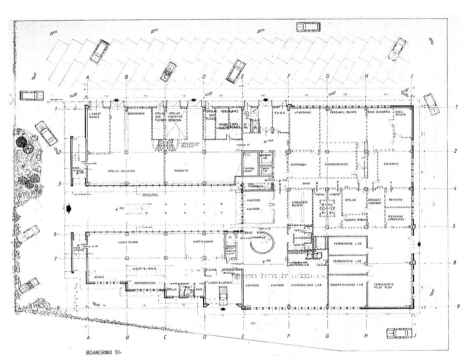

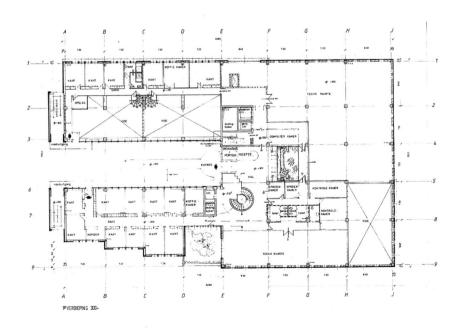

Detail of the rows of windows showing the
entrance at the end of the left facade.

View of the left facade.

wing and the offices in the right wing. The section of the
building which links the two wings is one half laboratories
and one half service areas.

The central area of the U shape was then enclosed
with a transparent vaulted roof which covers the whole
area up to the entrance at the end of the two wings. A
lively contrast is established by the transparent roof,
which projects out of the red brick structure and creates
an interior space flooded with natural light, providing an
area of repose and relaxation within the working
environment. An overhead footbridge facilitates
communication between labs and offices, contributes to
the vanishing line and facilitates maintenance work.

The next step was to design a front entrance and add
emergency stairs without disrupting the harmony of the

composition, an ensemble conditioned by the situation of
the transparent structure in the centre. The architectural
composition is based on breaking down the monolithic
volume, which is made lighter from the inside in an
attempt to convey a spatial dynamism which is based on
shapes and materials, but also on more ephemeral
elements such as natural light, shadows and artificial
light. The building and technological methods used were
industrial prefab components (assembled in the builder's
yard). The architect also used solid bricks, the normal
building material in Holland, to reinforce the relationship
between the new building and the surrounding
architectural context. Vertical and horizontal reinforced
concrete structures have been used together with joisted
floors and railings in prefabricated dry concrete. The

calculation of the primary and secondary steel structures gave sizes, and consequently weights, which were larger than expected (i.e. main girders with HEB 350 profiles and secondary beams with IPE 240 profiles). In order to resolve this problem the architect decided to use an extruded polycarbonate slab with a maximum thickness of 9 mm as the main structural element. The vaulted glass roof is 17 m wide and 28.20 m long, giving a total surface area of 700 m². This required a very complex design, and used all the technological know-how the architect had gained from the design of the IBG/General Electric buildings.

The lateral facade has a single entrance which leads into a small area slightly separate from the right wing, situated midway along the facade. A recess above the door is ornamented with plants. The windows are laid out in two clearly distinct blocks separated by this door. In the first block, which includes the area from the front facade up to the side entrance, the main characteristic is the vertical and rectangular distribution of the three upper floors, while the windows on the two lower floors are similar to those on the opposite facade. In the second block, the repetition of the square windows framed with bronze-coloured aluminium is varied by the inclusion of another type which resembles a honeycomb.

The rear facade of Eurocetus has a single entrance. Like the rest of the building, geometric and primarily straight lines clearly predominate over curves. On this

General view of Eurocetus seen from the right.

Elevation of the front facade.

Detail of the door on the front facade, showing the transparent roof.

View of the transparent roof from inside the
building.

Ground floor hall showing stairs leading to
the first floor.

facade the differences in the design and layout of the
windows is also repeated.

They are designed and distributed according to the
same criteria and forms. The logo and name of the
company have been included at each end of the upper
floor. In other ways, this facade is a continuation of the
design criteria which govern the execution of the external
appearance of the whole building. The most attractive
features of this project are on the main front facade. In
addition to being the prelude to the transparent roof,
instead of being treated as an orthodox opening, the
main entrance is an independent structure set in the
middle of the glass structure which links the two lateral
wings. The rectangular structure of the door, which fits in
well with the composition formed by the transparent roof

and facade, is slanted at an oblique angle creating a kind
of polyhedron. This gives the sensation of three-
dimensional relief within the block.

This main door leads into a hall decorated with plants
and a sculpture representing the company logo. The
interior furnishing and decoration was executed in local
wood and stone. Directly inside the door there is a
stairway leading to the first floor of the five levels in the
building. On either side of this staircase and behind it
there are offices and service areas crowned by the
transparent roof. There are two other ways of reaching
the upper floors: on the right a spiral staircase; on the
left a staff lift and service lift. These lifts are reached by
a kind of walkway at floor level which borders the
parquet.

Interior entrance.

Interior entrance and walkways.

The two wings linked by the transparent roof have four floors whereas the main building behind them is a five-storey structure. After climbing the staircase to reach the first level, visitors arrive at the interior entrance to the complex, composed of two folding doors. At this point two walkways connect with the wings, flanked by rows of windows giving onto the different rooms. This entrance leads into a small reception area. On the left of the reception, a second door gives access to the lifts and the laboratories on the first floor. On the right are the offices and other auxiliary areas and the spiral staircase. In front of the hall there is an interior patio with the plants. This area has adjustable partition walls which can be altered depending on the space required for the plants.

Obviously the laboratories are the key element in the complex; consequently, the design of this area was specially treated with regard to conditions of lighting and ventilation. It had to be naturally lit but shielded from direct light when possible. Internal curtains were unacceptable because of the need for an absolutely sterile environment, and external curtains were not considered suitable because of the weather and for maintenance reasons. The architect finally chose to use prefabricated brick lattices positioned 30 cm away from the contininuous facade. These were assembled in the builder's yard. The bricks were laid on a layer of binding mortar in order to create a system of ventilated facades. The natural ventilation of the tunnel is guaranteed by adjustable grids on the spine and by numerous air intakes on the front part of the building.

Detail of an office in the left wing.

View of the transparent roof and the different levels with walkways and access stairs to the first floor.

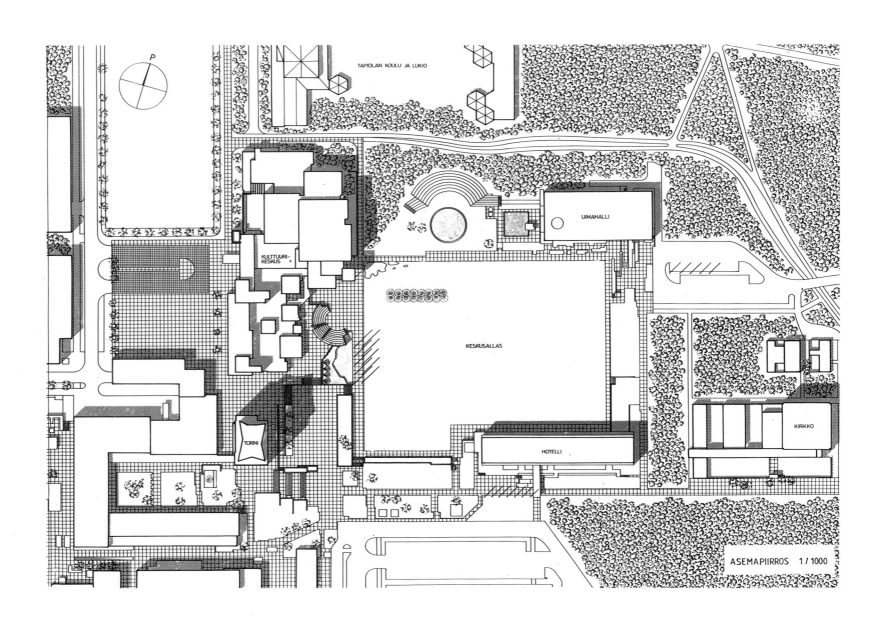

ASEMAPIIRROS 1 / 1000

22

Espoo Cultural Centre

Arto Sipinen

The construction of the cultural centre in the Finnish city of Espoo represents a new triumph in allying town planning and the functional architecture of today. With guidance from master architect Alvar Aalto, Arto Sipinen has introduced the constants of form and structure which characterize his work in this new building. There are certain similarities with another of his great projects, the Mikkeli Concert Hall, but the importance of this present work stems from how it fits in with the specific urban framework. However, although it is subordinate to this, it still maintains a character of independence and self-affirmation.

It has been included in the general town expansion scheme and this has influenced its location and relationship to the surrounding buildings. Espoo, the third largest city in Finland in terms of population and importance, has much to offer because of the many attractions of its natural landscape. The expansion of the city into the countryside has been accomplished with the typical respect that Finnish architecture holds for the environment and led to the creation of the Tapiola Garden City. It has become part of the cultural infrastructure channelling additional services that cater to tourism and the city itself.

The idea of having a cultural centre dates from the beginning of the fifties, and forms part of the detailed plan for the garden city designed by Aarne Ervi. The plan was to build a large theatre opposite the pool in the centre of the complex. Finally, in 1972, it was decided that a centre embracing a wide variety of cultural

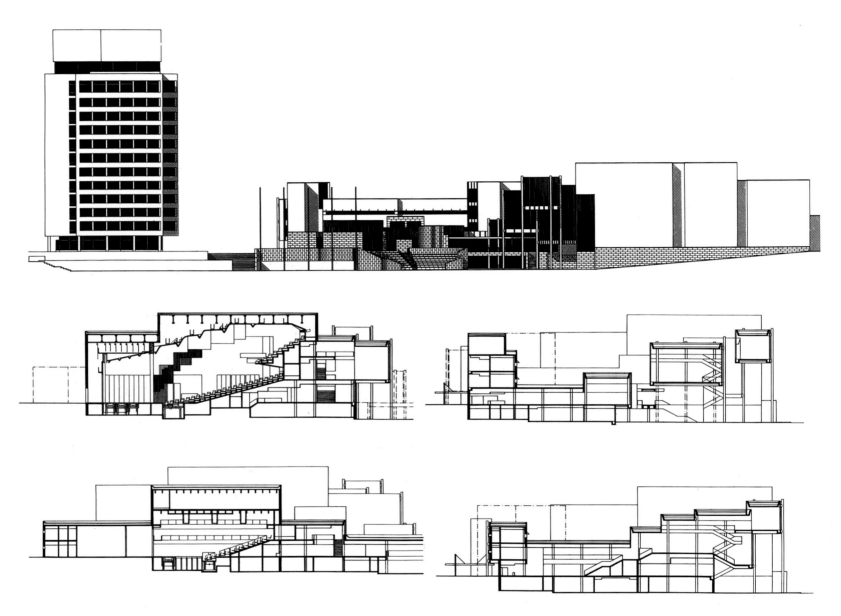

Sections of the buildings.

View of the lake area. The use of columns on the exterior makes for a lightness which contrasts with the bulk of the architectural structure.

Plan of the first floor.

Plan of the second floor.

White surfaces and glass make a perfect
match.

activities should be built. Arto Sipinen's Moonbridge
project was finally accepted in about 1980. Ervi located
his building to the north of the office block and to the
west of the large pool. The new construction would have
to take account of the huge site and form part of a
dialogue with the existing buildings.

Sipinen's architectural theories are primarily based on
building large blocks that crystallize, are superimposed
and contrast with each other to establish a functional
differentiation from the outside. This play on volumes has
to blend with the type of surrounding urban landscape.
The main building is located to the north of the new
complex. Complementary buildings are joined around it
on varying ground levels for the cultural activities offered
by the centre. The configuration and volumes had to

respond to the dictates of the buildings in front. Firstly
the new building was defined as a huge presence to
contrast with the flat expanse of the large pool. It would
also oppose the geometrically simple hotel designed by
Ervi to the south-east of the overall plan. Finally the
construction had to respect the emblematic importance
of the office block that was built in 1961 and had become
the symbol of the Tapiola Garden City.

The solutions that the project came up with to
respond to these conditions can be summed up,
respectively, in the shape of the huge volumetric mass
that stands out in both presence and complexity against
the artificial lake and the hotel, while at the same time
highlighting horizontal planes to counteract the vertical
tendency of the office block. The complex layout of the

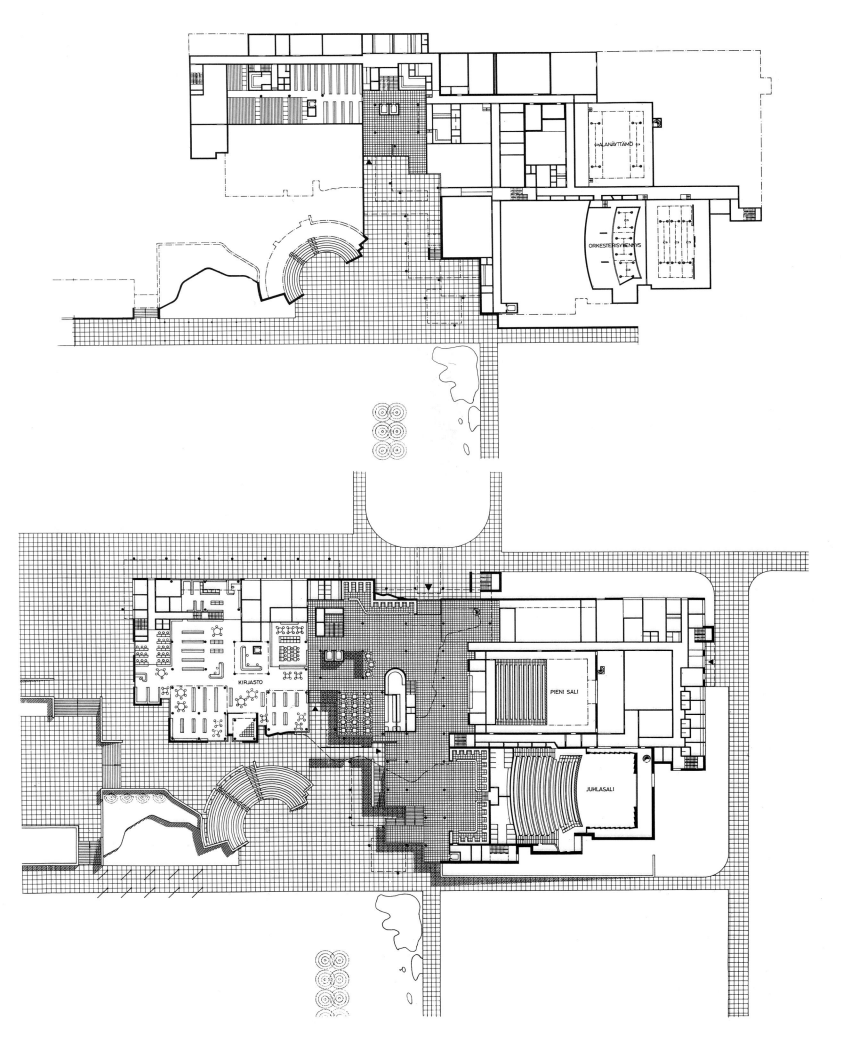

The massive columns rise straight out of the ground, taking the form of ascending cylinders.

volumes and blocks was devised for both functional diversity and the need to create an imposing image to help disguise the flat structure. The plan of the building is laid out not only to suit its urban environment, but also the beauty of the natural landscape in which it is set.

The site of the new building has a surface area of 12,900 m² and spatial capacity of 68,700 m³. The exterior has been largely influenced by suggestions from Aalto, the master architect. The large white masses distributed at different heights and the play on diaphanous glass boxes supported on stylized columns are characteristic of the architecture of both architects. The areas that have the fewest openings are placed facing west, whereas the large glass structures face east to capture the light and clarity for an optimum visual sequence.

The layout of the functional plan can initially be seen from the outside of the building. The large central volumes contain two concert halls, while behind the glass facades there are lobbies, reception, exhibition rooms and a cafeteria-restaurant. The south wing has a more stratified structure to house the cultural facilities: library, workers' and music institutes. There is a small open amphitheatre on the south-eastern side which produces a change in level. This is rectified by a raised platform which is reached by steps from the south and completes the design of this small terrace. This sector is able to provide for a number of cultural events. The interplay between the small waterfalls on one side and the large lake becomes a device for producing different tones of light.

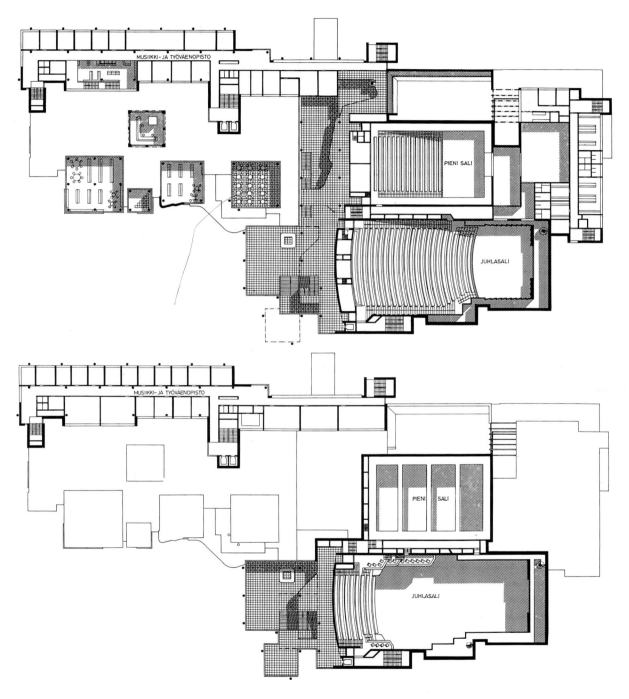

First and second floors of the other building.

The white of the exterior continues, but
slightly darker, in the interior.

The building is structurally organized on three floors.
The entrances to these go in two different directions. The
main entrance is situated on the western facade facing
the road, and has parking for 670 vehicles. From here
one enters directly into the exhibition hall that leads on to
the other rooms. There is also access by way of the
platform mentioned above, situated at the junction
between the cafeteria and the entrance lobby, to the
large concert hall.

The first floor of the cultural centre is on the same
level as the central pool. The varying levels mean that
part of this area is underground and used for storage
purposes and maintenance installations, or rehearsal
rooms for music and dance. The main entrance to the
building is on the first floor and leads to corridors that
communicate with the rest of the building. The ground
plan includes the ticket and information offices, a
cafeteria seating 80 people, the library that has both
adults and children's sections, the entrance lobbies to
the smaller hall and additional rooms for performers.

The door to the main hall is on the second floor in a
large glassed-in gallery on the eastern side of the building.
On the opposite side, in the southern section, there are
rooms for music classes and rehearsal rooms next to the
administration offices and the workers' institute. On the
top floor there is the entrance to the circle of the large
concert hall, located on another glassed-in blacony which
is strategically placed for a good view. Here, too, there are
additional areas used by the two institutes.

The main hall is called the Tapiola Hall and has seating

Cylinders are a recurring feature, from lights
to banister rails and tables.

for an audience of 812, of which 199 are in the circle
upstairs. It has been built to cater for large perfomances:
musicals, operas, orchestras or choirs. The high acoustic
quality – with a 2.0-second reverberation timing –
is the result of recent collaboration with Alpo Halme.
Stage equipment and lighting are controlled from a room
at the back of the hall, with a separate projection room.
The stage measures 16 x 12 m, and can be adapted to a
variety of different kinds of events by covering the pit
with an apron electrically operated from the back which
extends the stage area to 265 m². Ventilation, lighting
and other equipment for holding congresses and
conferences are also housed in this area which has a
capacity of 9,300 m³.

The smaller Louhi Hall, designed for events on a
smaller scale, is also well equipped. It provides seating
for between 300 to 442 and has a surface area of 300 m².
A series of balconies are also available placed to run
parallel down the sides of the hall. Its acoustic facilities
are regulated from a control room at the back of the hall
in the same way as the larger hall.

The exterior of the building is clad in large blocks of
quartz sandstone and glass and it has slab paving.
Inside, the light enters from all sides through huge clear
glass windows; the walls, too, are extremely light,
entirely panelled in birchwood and the area is decorated
with plants. The same wood is used for the floors,
together with travertine marble and mosaic. Furniture for
the general public is aesthetically elegant and functional,
and has been designed by Alvar Aalto himself.

The whole design is indebted to the grand Finnish master architect. Sipinen has reinterpreted the fundamental concepts and offers an architectural work that maintains an uninterrupted dialogue with the buildings that are already there, in terms of form as well as scale. Integration and a relationship with the surrounding natural environment is another of the architect's basic objectives. He has achieved a construction that, through the interplay of presence and space, transparency and opacity, is ideal as a cultural and entertainment venue.

View of the centre's lecture theatre.

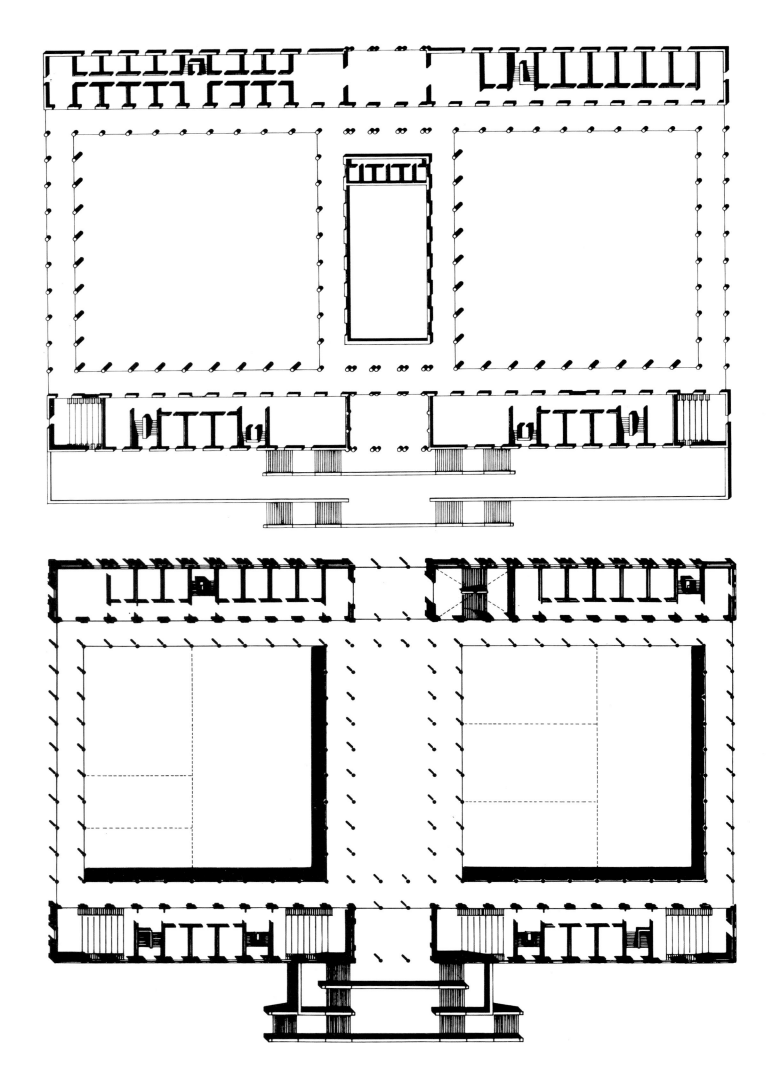

Plan of one of the floors in the INEF complex.

Plan of the ground floor.

The INEF building

Ricardo Bofill (Taller de Arquitectura)

The celebration of the Olympic Games in Barcelona in 1992 stimulated the construction of a number of architectural works in this Mediterranean capital. These projects were heterogeneous in nature, as were the diverse tendencies represented by all the architects and engineers who undertook the challenge of transforming the Olympic city. The fact that the Olympic Games is primarily a sporting event did not necessarily mean that all the new construction was directly related to sport. This is clearly demonstrated by the ambitious town planning projects, such as the construction of a new system of ring roads, and other projects related to telecommunications such as the Foster and Calatrava towers.

Born in Barcelona in 1939, Ricardo Bofill studied at the Escuela Técnica Superior de Arquitectura de

Barcelona (1955-56), and subsequently in the University of Architecture in Genoa (1957-1960). On graduating, he founded the Taller de Arquitectura based in Barcelona (with a team composed of Peter Hodgkinson, J. Pierre Carniaux, Patrick Genard, Rogelio Giménez, Fernando Trueba, José María Rocias, Paul Elliot, Rosaria Iacovino, Xavier Grau and Omar Migiliore), which later opened offices in Paris and New York. The history of this practice is studded with triumphs in very prestigious competitions: ADI-FAD (Barcelona, 1964), the Fritz Schumacher Award from the University of Hamburg (1968), International Design Award from the American Society of Interior Designers (1978), and the first prize in the competition for the construction of the Balcon-sur-la-Ville housing development in Dreux, France (1981).

Elevation of the south facade.

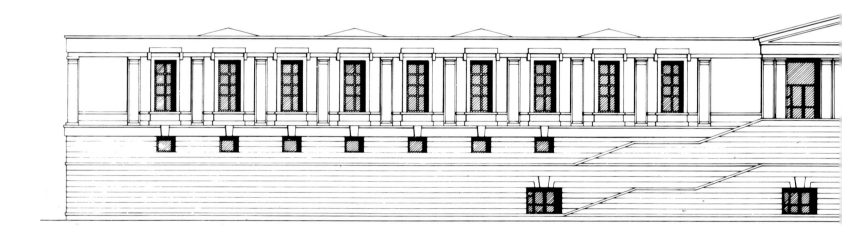

The firm directed by Bofill can be described as a multidisciplinary group interested in many facets of creative activity. The cornerstone of their philosophy is a personal vision of the Modern Movement whose functionalism they considered necessary but insufficient. After a period of architectural research and experimentation with constructive forms (the Walden 7 and Sant Gregori apartment blocks in Barcelona), Bofill entered a phase marked by experimentation with symbols and concepts, which took on a somewhat neoclassical flavour. He has been responsible for a large number of works, and has gained international recognition, especially in France. In recent years, Bofill has focused his attention on the architectural, urban and cultural modernisation of his native city where, in addition to the expansion of the airport, he has carried out a series of projects such as the National Institute of Physical Education Building (INEF), the National Theatre of Catalonia and the Institute of Mediterranean Studies.

This building is located on Montjuïc hill in Barcelona (95 metres above sea level) and forms part of the Olympic complex. The situation gave rise to the idea of integrating the large volume of the container into the surrounding landscape without, however, allowing this to become an obstacle to the transmission of the desired sensation, that of a modern work in a classical monumentalist tradition. Given that classicism is inevitably linked to proportion, the Taller de Arquitectura wanted to achieve a balance between the construction and the landscape by using advanced technology based on the use of prefabricated elements made of architectural concrete of a colour similar to that of the stones of the mountain itself.

The site has a sharp north-south slope which was used in the plan to accommodate two floors on the northern side and four on the south. The fact that this is an educational building helped to alleviate one of the difficulties associated with the design of sports pavilions, which is that the size of the sporting installations invariably dwarfs the area housing the auxiliary support services, and tends, therefore, to impose an extremely functional and utilitarian image upon the whole building. This work is very unusual in this respect and differs from what was considered to be an ideal architectural

language for the emblematic context of Montjuïc.

In this design, the south-facing facade of the teaching block (which features a large stairway leading down to the playing fields) together with the administration block on the northern side, absorb and effectively conceal most of the sports halls, which are nine metres high. The east and west facades, on the other hand, are open galleries, glassed-in arcades which provide daylight for the activities in the patios and halls. Thus, the whole volume is treated as a homogeneous continuity rather than as a collection of volumes of different sizes.

The centre of all social activity is the main entrance hall, which overlooks the two competition areas situated on a lower level. To the south, there is an open porch

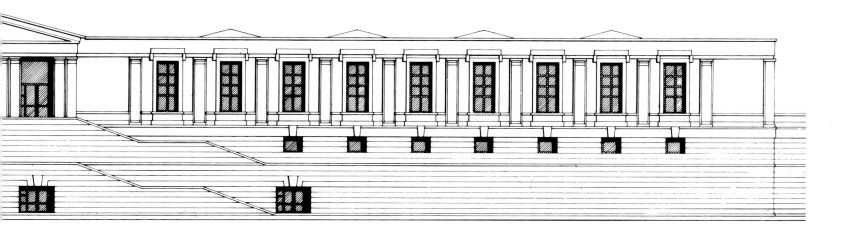

The steep slope has been used to accommodate two floors on the north side and four on
the south side.

The large windows all around the INEF building provide ample daylight inside the building.

The prefabricated concrete blocks used to face the construction fit in well with the surrounding buildings.

and a lookout terrace from which a flight of steps leads down to the playing fields. These steps are an ideal spot for students and visitors to sit and chat, watch the games or simply enjoy the sunshine. The bar and restaurant are located below these stairs where there is also a separate entrance to the library. The library has a single large and informal room for reading and several others which are used for viewing videos and other activities. The upper floor is completely occupied by the changing rooms which are connected directly to the sports halls, which can be accessed from the sides and the mezzanine floor. The swimming pool is housed in a separate building on the east side, connected to the Faculty Building by the base wall and a pergola on the circular explanade of the Plaça d'Europa.

Above the changing rooms, at the back of the main level of the hall, are the classrooms, conference rooms and seminar rooms facing south, and the teachers' rooms, offices, video production rooms and laboratories on the north side. The people circulating through the galleries have an uninterrupted view of the competition areas where the sporting activities studied in the classrooms are put into practice. These patios can be divided into different spaces – visually and physically – through the use of acoustic curtains. The light lower roof acts as a controlled source of natural light and also as a base for all the artificial lighting and the public address systems.

The Taller chose to use an architectural and landscaping language clearly associated with noucentisme, a romantic

The serene appearance of the INEF building is
the result of the architect's neoclassical
style.

*and eclectic neoclassicism, which is the common style of
the other buildings in the area. Bofill and his team chose
to purify these classical intentions and to use advanced
modern technology, in this case prefabricated stone
panels (architectural concrete), decorated with minimalist,
conceptual relief. The result is a very sober modern
construction, integrated into the visual context, which is
an example of beautiful harmony. For example, the parti
of the columns around the competition rooms which
support the roof and the connecting galleries between
the interior facade and these pillars, generates a pattern
of composition in proportion to the vertical planes of the
windows, doors, columns, and pilasters. The interior
facade, on the other hand, is treated as an urban
frontispiece and clad with the prefabricated stone panels.*

*The horizontal lines resulting from the difference in the
number of floors on the north and south sides produce a
two-floor basement with a simple line of columns above,
which encircle the whole building, culminating in a frieze
around the copper roof.*

*The architects have tried to use the most pure and
simple materials possible. However, the volume of work
demanded high perfomance and consequently higher
costs. Prefabricated stone of the light sandy colour of the
native Montjuïc rock provides a contrasting backdrop to
the lacquered aluminium window frames glazed with
reflective smoked glass. All the terraces and stairs are
paved with artificial stone slab; the interior floors are
varnished wood parquet, cork or ceramic tiles; the walls
are plaster or have been finished with fabric or wood. All*

The spaciousness of the interior is one of
the agreeable features of this work.

The plate glass windows provide the gym with plenty of natural light.

The indoor competition areas can be observed by the people using the connecting galleries.

the ceilings are insulated with light, sandy-coloured, acoustic panels, alternated in a modular system with panes of glass which diffuses the natural light. The ceilings also house all the supplementary connections installed behind lacquered aluminium grids specially designed for this project.

The open-air playing fields are an extension of the building and the result of the same geometry. There is a large grass field in the middle, bordered by two small wooded spaces for parking. This is complemented by a hard tennis court and a hard hockey pitch. All these spaces are situated on a raised area of ground surrounded by a hedge and typical Mediterranean trees.

The plate glass, punctuated with columns, continues around the interior of the building to create an open-plan effect.

The columns, which are a feature of the interior, are an example of the classical design.

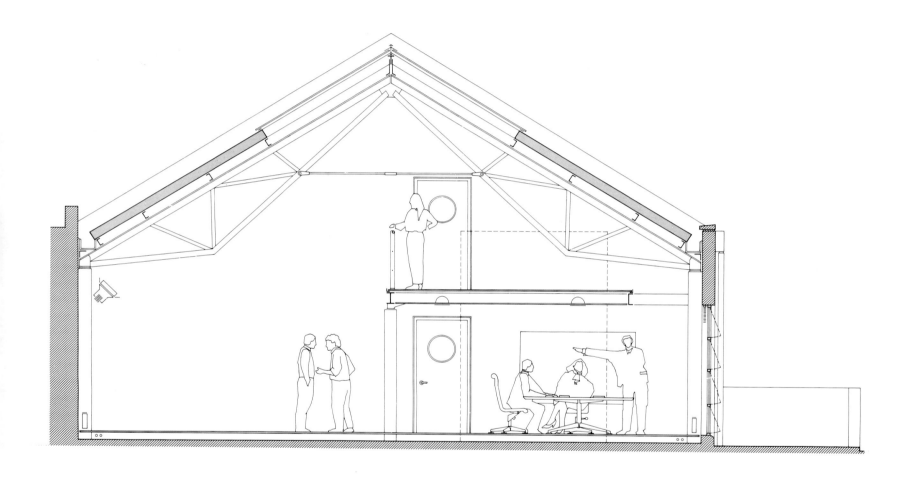

Elevation.

Colebrooke Place

Troughton McAslan

Much of the brilliant work of these two British architects has been in the field of large public buildings. Their vast theoretical and historical knowledge of architecture underlines an enlightened idiom that combines respect for the achievements of the modern movement with the most up-to-date technological developments. Their projects bear the signs of an obvious evolution, in which the number of structural components are reduced and the expressive content increased without recourse to exaggeration or mannerism. The rational conception implicit in their typological language by no means excludes imagination and inventiveness from their proposals.

In Colebrooke Place, Troughton and McAslan, planning on a smaller scale than that of their usual projects, concentrated their efforts and drew on their experience to create a studio in a smaller space. Colebrooke Place represents another milestone in a type of planning they initiated in 1984 with Design House, continued four years later with St. Peter's Street, and which culminates in this project. The characteristics observable in their large-scale constructions are also evident in these smaller buildings. The first of these projects involved a more extensive use of advanced technology, the second was based on rigour and strength, while Colebrooke Place tends more toward simplification and abstraction.

Like the neighbouring St. Peter's Street, this new project shows how a small, existing building lacking in quality can be transformed into an area with wide spatial

Interior view of the building. The combination of warm and cold materials – the wooden floor and metal ceiling – endow it with great balance.

Plan of the building.

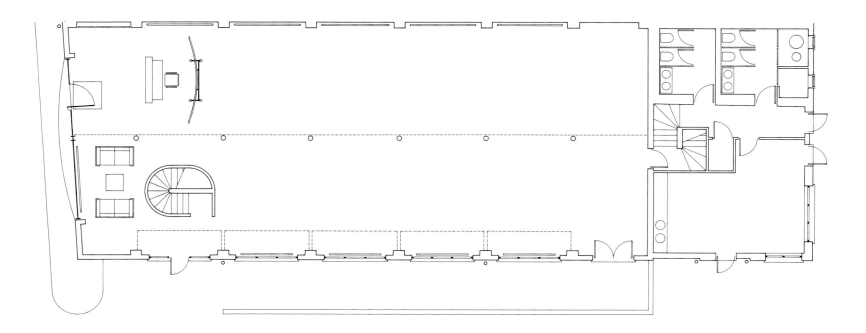

perspectives and a warm, comfortable interior. The original structure, a warehouse built in the fifties, was poorly planned and executed. The project involved remodelling and rehabilitating the old structure and introducing a functional programme that would suit its new purpose. The original warehouse is divided into two areas. The first consists of private rooms and offices housed in a small block in the rear of the ground plan. The second area, the large main studio, is the significant space of the structure.

The entire expressive power of the project is concentrated in this studio. One of the problems confronting the architects was the low budget. But instead of limiting them, these economic restrictions only served to spur their imagination and ingenuity. Thus, the

work methodology which underlies the logic of their elegant and creative solutions can be more clearly appreciated. Due to urban growth, countless antiquated, unusable buildings have been remodelled outside and inside and made serviceable again. In this case, with the limited financial resources available, the rehabilitation process was a more viable and natural option than building anew.

The small dimensions and prexisting configuration defined a volume which set the tone of the project. The architects could only follow the geometric laws dictated by the original shell. The task was to increase the visual perspective and to give the building a sense of spaciousness. To achieve this it was necessary to introduce elements that would order the different

On the top floor, the simple furnishings blend in perfectly with their surroundings.

Detail of the glass roof.

functions and at the same time preserve the best visual perspective. The interior volume was to be read as a whole, and thus dividing elements received a dynamic and flexible treatment.

The most suitable solution was the construction of an intermediate level, taking advantage of the heightened perspective of the angular roof. This new masonry platform reorganizes the interior, with a lower level occupying the entire surface of the ground plan, and the one above it only half. The creation of a two-storey interior solved the problem of communication with the annex block, which has the same dual structuring, through their symmetrically placed doors. The distributing platform is supported by a line of widely spaced columns, which illustrate the simplicity of the approach and the

execution. The conventional metal railing with a stylized handrail and supports finished in black reinforce the visual link between the two levels. No element blocks the continuous visual perspective. The separations are light, barely suggested, and the planes divide the space in a clear, transparent manner.

Two other structural components serve as distribution elements. The first is located in the area beneath the floor slab of the intermediate level and consists of an oval screen that is open at one end. Its purpose is to conceal the stairway that connects the two floors physically. The use of canvas provided a highly plastic and, most importantly, a very economical solution. The other distribution element is a sliding partition, also made of canvas. It is situated in the two-storey space at a variable distance from the entrance and serves to reorder the view of the premises from that entrance and to form a small reception area. It is a metal structure on small wheels with a stretcher system to support the fabric. The use of partitions is a cheap and imaginative technical resource that Troughton and McAslan exploited in one of their large complexes, Apple Computers, UK.

The rehabilitation of the interior included the solution of several problems related to the roofing. Its angular structure is reinforced by a group of exposed steel beams, whose thrusts are in different directions. There are large, central skylight areas, with glazing that follows the form of the roof. The metal window frames are a simple solution to the need for fast, inexpensive execution. The glass allows natural light to enter the interior, creating a transparent, diaphanous space, which makes the studio appear larger.

In this way, the interior remodelling reflects the external treatment of the building. In addition to reconditioning the preexisting structures, the architects had to consider the positions of the entrances and openings that link the studio with the urban setting, their goal being to catch the greatest possible amount of light and to create a functional work space. The glazing was given a special treatment to prevent a substantial penetration of strong light in such a small interior, which would have been a hindrance to the work carried out in the studio. Acid etching makes the glass translucent and

Structures merge and interplay to form the body of the building.

Interior with Bauhaus-style furnishings.

the light that enters is diffused and indirect. The front elevation has two large quadrangular openings, one of which is the transparent glass door of the main entrance. The side elevations have numerous windows that begin at floor level, and several additional entrances. The rear volume is cubical with a flat roof and is dominated by the same colour contrast.

The simple tones and textures of the materials used in the exterior are repeated in the interior. Brick painted white, glass that lets in indirect natural light, the oak flooring and the fabric partitions all respond to a use of colour that creates a diaphanous, transparent atmosphere. The group of columns supporting the floor slab of the intermediate level, in grey with dark nuances, and the black railing contradict the overall environment.

The furniture also represents somewhat of a contrast to the established tone and is characterized by an extreme functionalism that does not preclude an elegant, aesthetic quality. To the left of the main door there is a waiting area formed by two simply designed sofas on metal frameworks with a small table between them. The ventilation and artificial lighting systems are handled through a simple installation of ventilators at the point where the wall and the roof meet, and a line of spotlights. The small number of structural and functional components and the simplicity of the way they are used illustrate extensive achievements with a great economy of means. Thus, the architecture is rational but at the same time replete with expressive power.

The second floor rests on broad elliptical pillars.

General view of the exterior.

The metal structures provide a feeling of lightness.

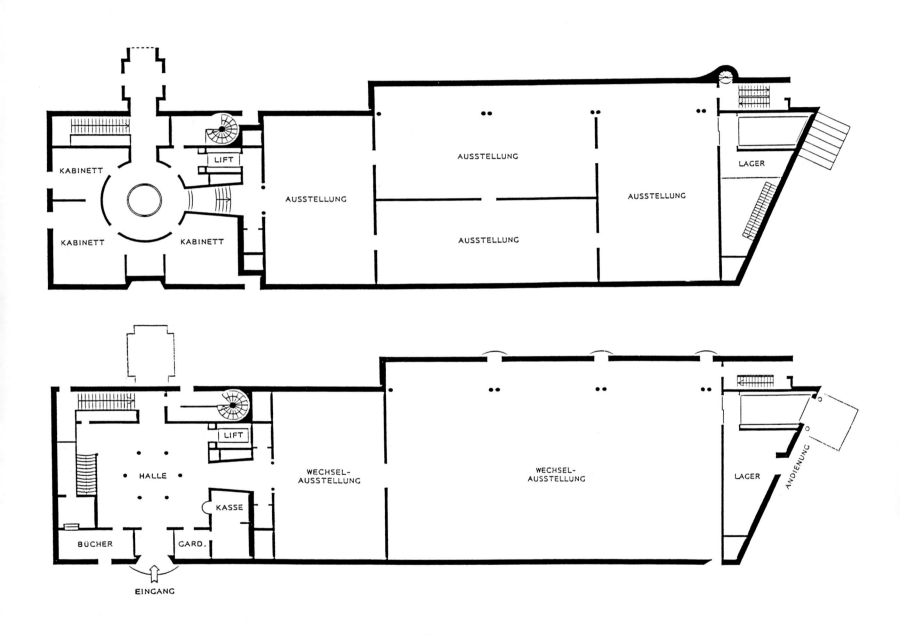

KABINETT

KABINETT · KABINETT

LIFT

AUSSTELLUNG

AUSSTELLUNG

AUSSTELLUNG

AUSSTELLUNG

AUSSTELLUNG

LAGER

LIFT

HALLE

KASSE

BÜCHER · GARD.

EINGANG

WECHSEL-
AUSSTELLUNG

WECHSEL-
AUSSTELLUNG

LAGER

ANDIENUNG

Städel Museum

Gustav Peichl

The process of urban and cultural development in Frankfurt has recently achieved a further triumph with the construction of the new extension wing for the Städel Museum. The museum tradition that has taken shape along the banks of the River Main, on the Schaumainkai, has been visibly improved by the work of the Viennese architect Gustav Peichl, who took advantage of the existing structure to demonstrate a logical continuity, both modern and comprehensible, without having to resort to mere formal and conceptual imitation. The new extension harmonises perfectly with the original forms and series of exterior spaces that become complementary features of the architectural language. The latter was constrained by the functional requirements, since the entire design is aimed at enhancing contemplation and

was, in effect, a conscious search for space and light. These are the two fundamental criteria on which the architect based his project.

The Städel Art Institute, founded in 1816 at the same time as the school, is a private organisation which, in 1906, merged with the Municipal Gallery, whose collection covers a wide range of works of art dating from the fourteenth century up to the present day. The urgent need to construct a new building to hold twentieth-century works, along with temporary exhibitions, gave rise to a restricted competition in 1987. The prospective building had to fulfil a series of requirements that combined functional and aesthetic criteria and harmonised with the urban and natural surroundings.

The museum is situated on the eastern corner of

53

Plan of the floor of the museum.

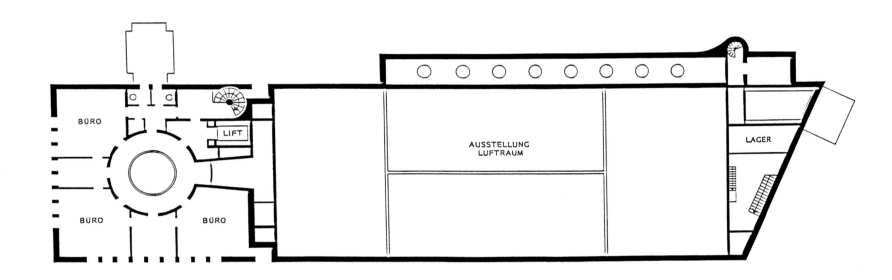

Holbeinstrasse, between the institute and the Städel
School. The extension had to conform with the character
of the street and correspond to the scale and style of its
buildings. By the same token, it was necessary to provide
a public footpath which, via the sculpture garden, linked
Steinlesstrasse with Städelstrasse and connected the two
enclosures. Among the proposed specifications was the
need to conserve the listed monuments and establish a
new architectural form which did not overshadow them,
but acted simply as a continuation. The project had to be
subordinated to the principle of contemplation, based on
the concepts of wall, space and light. The competition
also specified that between the existing courtyard to the
west of the buildings and the exhibition courtyard
situated on the eastern corner, a park area be created, on

as large a scale as possible, linking both exteriors.

The conditions set out by the museum committee
took shape in the design submitted by Gustav Peichl, the
eventual winner. The judges took into account the
simplicity and the high degree of the harmonious
elements in the project, which presented a substantially
modern architectural work that economised on design
effects. The facades, based on the appearance of the
garden wall, the smooth form of the roof with its skylights
and the division of the masses of the building into a head
and a longer body were the main factors in the
judgement. The project for extending the Städel School
and the relationship between both buildings was also
highly thought of.

The architect's first thoughts about the design were

concerned with the peculiarities and difficulties predetermined by the shape and height of the building, the limited space for construction work and the exact layout of the grounds, which left no open border. Peichl's project was therefore confined to coordinating the different functional areas of the museum and the form of the exterior. A simple, ordered and functional design was chosen, with an entrance or head building to distribute the space. This section, independent in form, was called the Villa to accentuate its small size and achieve the desired proportions.

The extension responded more to functional planning criteria than to an ambitious design project. The forms of the exterior facades were conceived from visual and

cultural hypotheses appropriate to a building of this nature. This was achieved by the choice of materials and by the clean lines and lack of excessive adornment.

The conflict generated by the continuous confrontation beetween aesthetics and functional aspects, beauty and practicability, were resolved as a result of the method of distribution. The new block was set out on a rectangular ground plan with an angled wall at one end, which gives it a trapezoidal shape. Several of the interior layouts have been translated to the exterior, and consequently the elevation acquires some extremely effective reliefs.

All tendencies towards impersonal, provisional modernity or imitation were eliminated in the treatment of

Detail of the roof of the museum.

Plan of one of the exhibition rooms.

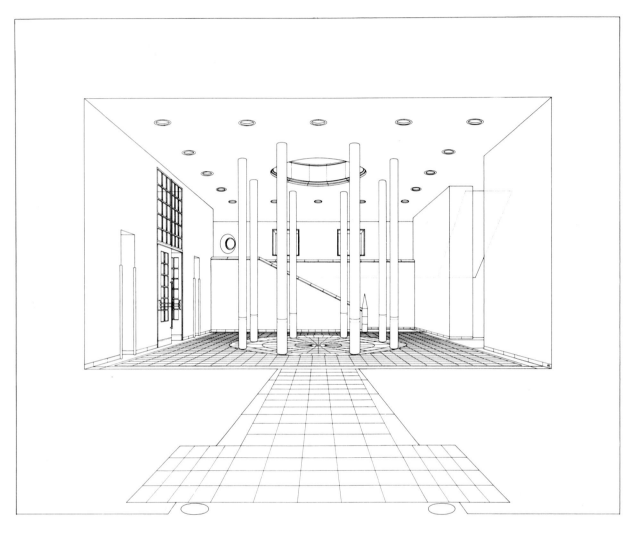

the facades. On the contrary, the architect tried to create an impression of solidity and discretion, without ignoring the expressive potential and the desire to illustrate the cultural character of the work. In the main section, running parallel to Holbeinstrasse, the intention was to suggest a division of the functions (the exhibition area and the head element) by means of a slit in the side walls of the intersection point. Similarly, on the facades adjoining the sculpture garden, another superimposed feature with the same geometrical characteristics stands out from the main volume. On this turn a half cylinder has been placed, which emerges with great elegance and sharpness from the wall. This conforms with the spiral staircase which links the first and second floors of the building.

The sharp, clean lines of the exterior are reinforced by this play between the projecting shapes. The contrast between the straight and curved forms, the absence of openings, the angle of the back facade and other features such as the glass pyramid which serves as a kind of canopy are the most representative elements of the building and give it a contained tension which has an undeniable impact on the mind of the onlooker. By using an exquisite white sandstone, and a much darker socle, the feeling of serenity and restraint is recaptured. Both factors complement each other in a blend of simplicity and moderation which exemplify the cultural requirements of the construction.

The interior architecture also had to meet the demands set out in the funcional brief. The building is laid out on four levels, one of which is below ground. The entrance is on Holbeinstrasse and opens out into the reception area, which is distinguished by the stairway with balustrade that leads to the first floor, the oval window, a recess to sit and contemplate an overall view of the museum and the temporary exhibition area. This simple layout and the use of special materials such as chequered stone tiling, the old-fashioned stucco of the walls and the circle of white columns provide the lobby with a pleasing and inviting character. The diversity of the materials (natural stone, metal and oak) and their gleaming, even texture, which is easy to maintain, appeal to both the eye and the touch.

The eye-shaped opening in the ceilings of all the levels draws the overhead light from the roof and

distributes it evenly throughout the interior. On the upper levels, the circle appears to be surrounded by curved walls which form several cabinets used for exhibiting small format pieces. From here one gets the best vertical perspective, with the exquisite chequered tile floor of the lobby and the skylight in the roof. The square-circle contrast and the classically inspired structure and configuration of the ground plan create an atmosphere of well-being that is most appropriate to the contemplation of art. The form, proportions and symmetry serve the functional aims of the building and facilitate the orientation of the visitor, an essential element for any museum.

To differentiate between the permanent collection and temporary exhibitions, they were laid out on different

Detail of the main door showing the rows of small windows that decorate the façade.

Detail of one of the corners of the façade.

View across one of the rooms. The whiteness and the plentiful light give the museum a sense of space.

Looking down into one of the rooms in the museum. The black and white tiling follows a chessboard pattern.

Interior of one of the rooms. Also visible are
some of the pictures on display.

levels. The former was installed on the upper levels and the latter, on the mezzanine floor. The design of the rooms was intended to make the walls, light and space symbolise the essential aspects of a museum. The areas that determine the general outline of the extension have been divided into four rooms that are generous in size and well connected. The exits to the sculpture garden are intrinsic to an appreciation of the interior and link the exterior courtyards with the ground-floor exhibition room. Both the centrally located circular rooms and the spacious exhibition sections were conceived as areas where the largest possible number of paintings could be hung. All of which, along with the defined visual axes and the high, slim entrance apertures, create a calm

atmosphere that attempts to avoid any kind of excessive formalism which might distract the visitor from the real centre of attention, the works of art. The architecture of the museum is subordinate in a natural and elegant way to the ideal concept of contemplation.

The process of extending the Städel Museum could be considered an exercise in a clear and simple style, in which there is no lack of present-day architectural language – simply measured proportions. The classical layout of the building is noticeably affected by certain extremely well-fashioned features such as the cylindrical projection and angle of the facades. The contrast between the curved and straight lines is also made evident in the interior as well as the delicate and very

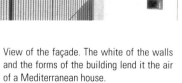

View of the façade. The white of the walls and the forms of the building lend it the air of a Mediterranean house.

expressive use of durable and contemporary materials. The complex aims to harmonise both the surrounding physical area and the cultural elements of its function as a museum and achieves it by an architectural continuity that on no occasion degenerates into mere imitation of existing buildings.

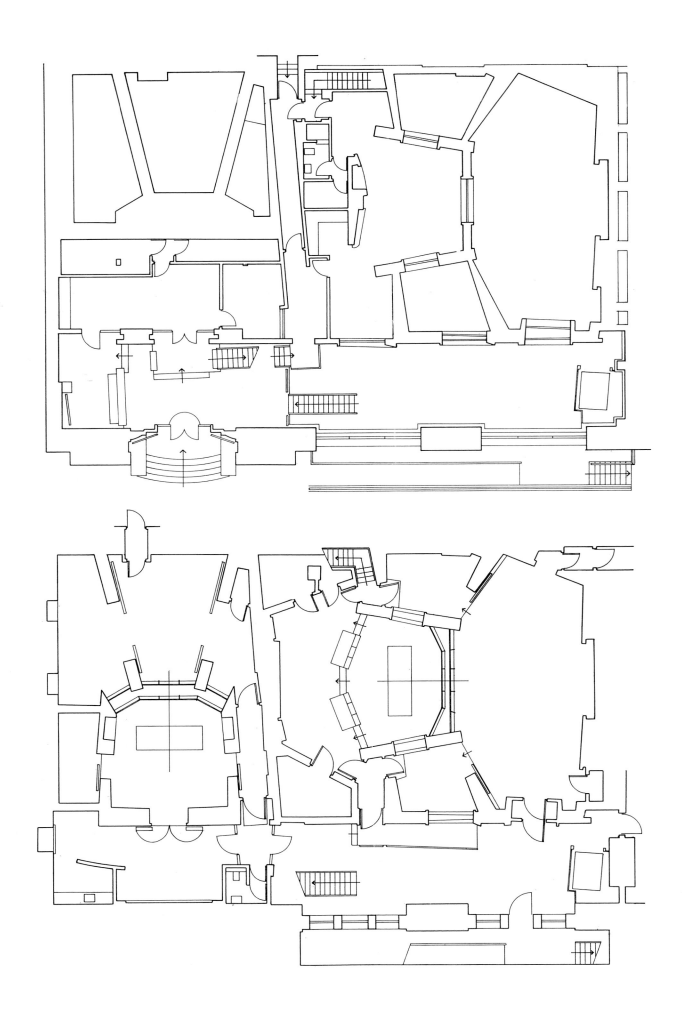

Recording Studio Metropolis

Powell-Tuck, Connor & Orefelt

The Metropolis project provided the Powell-Tuck, Connor & Orefelt firm with an ideal opportunity to execute a masterly synthesis of architecture, interior design, technology and functional programming. The intervention entailed the remodelling of an existing structure in which the satisfaction of the various new needs had to be compatible with the architectural style. The architects chose to create an interior shell large enough to contain all of the equipment and installations (the acoustical, in particular) without resorting to any change in the original structures. Once the insulation process was completed, it was possible to introduce new sections and to articulate them according to the criteria of spatial flexibility and visual and physical communication. The result is a combination of high-tech architecture and the practicality of the pure design, of the functional, luminous public spaces and those like the studios that call for greater privacy.

The former Chiswick power station was designed by William Curtis Green toward the end of the nineteenth century and went into operation in 1901, providing electricity for the new tram service in west London. In 1911 it was finally closed down. In 1975, political opposition in the neighbourhood prevented the conversion of the building into a bus depot. Nine years later, the businessman Jonathan Wicks was interested in converting the old structure into a modern film studio. In 1985, after much controversy regarding its administration and financing, permission was obtained for a mixed development of nineteen blocks of flats, several office

Axonometric drawing of the studio.

General view showing the internal division
of space into levels.

Axonometric detail of the interior.

The layout of the interior is arranged as a series of modules centred around a metal staircase.

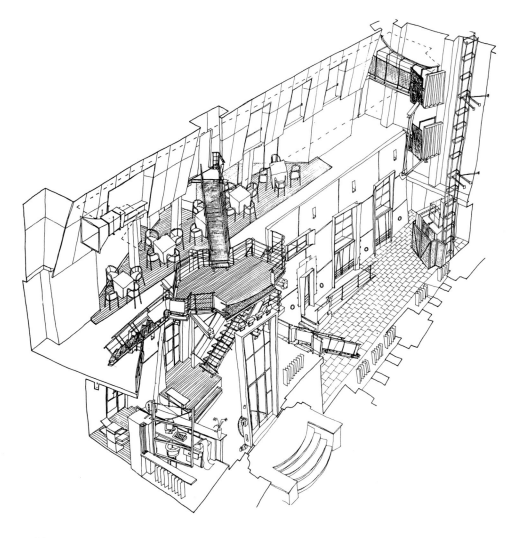

Axonometric section of one side of the studio.

The use of wood for flooring and walls provides a touch of warmth.

buildings, a car park and the recording studio. With the exception of the latter premises, the complex was executed by David Clarke Associates.

In 1986 Metropolis Studios Ltd. received the permits to construct the recording studio in the remaining space. In a limited competition, the commission was awarded to Powell-Tuck, Connor & Orefelt in October, the same year the plans were submitted. The project was executed in three phases due to the difficulties posed by the existing structure. The first two phases consisted in the construction of studios A and B which was terminated in May 1989, while the third phase, consisting of three new spaces, was completed in June 1990. Carey Taylor, the man who had financed and managed the operation,

stated clearly from the outset that his intention was to build the most important and up-to-date recording studio in Europe, and the end result fulfilled these expectations.

The site of the old power station is on Chiswick High Road, one of the main traffic arteries of west London. The complex consists of a large volume in Edwardian Gothic style, executed in brick and Porland stone, whose main facade has five huge archways. The introduction of an innovative, advanced technological programme posed a series of interior conflicts to be resolved without destroying the architectural value of the exterior within the urban fabric.

These difficulties were very diverse in nature. In the first place, the original stuctures had to be fully

Interior view from the top of the studio.

View of the stair that connects second and
third level.

respected, which ruled out any modification of the
facades or the roof. Secondly, the proximity of a group of
residential buildings (the nineteen blocks of flats that
directly faced the studios and those buildings on nearby
Merton Avenue) made a rigorous acoustical control
imperative. In addition to these external formal
constraints, there were also the considerations that are
common to any interior design, such as the distribution
and organization of space and the need for light in the
more public areas. In this case, the specific concerns
were with the sound quality and the conditions of security
and privacy required for the famous clientele.

To solve the essentially architectural problems related
to the urban context, the PTCO plan entailed the creation
of an interior volume in the form of vast modern premises

that reached the limits imposed by the old structure, but
did not come into contact with the walls. This strategy is
essentially a building within a building, which ensures a
natural distribution of the new programme without
modifying the existing outer surface. The new structure is
of reinforced concrete with a base that is independent of
the original brick and stone. On this new base the
architects were able to plan with complete autonomy and
freedom, since the extreme thickness of the materials
used acted as an acoustical screen for the neighbouring
apartment buildings.

The new internal shell not only offered acoustical
protection, but also initiated a stimulating dialogue
between the traditional and the contemporary. In
planning the interior as a huge concrete box, the contrast

A combination of warm and cold materials.

The furnishings chosen for the studio underscore the contrast of warmth and cold.

between the exterior warmth of the sound ceramic brick with its huge archways and the coldness of the new elements (of the structure and of the communications systems) its one of the most successful aesthetic achievements of the new premises. In addition, the architects controlled the potential for interior natural light, leaving spaces open according to the requirements of the programme.

The interior of the old power station is organized on four large surfaces, ordered in such a way as to make maximum use of the available space and to facilitate the physical, visual and acoustical relationships of the interior. Two entrances are located on the Chiswick High Road level, the first preceded by a flight of steps parallel to the main facade that provides access to the basement,

where the first phases of the project were executed. Because these installations would be put into operation before the entire project was completed, the initial stage was moved to this underground level. The basement houses the two large studios, A and B, and the floor of the large atrium that dominates the interior of the premises.

The second entrance at street level has a small curved ascending flight of steps in one of the glazed archways of the original facade. On the ground floor there are various reception areas and administrative offices. The interior structures are articulated around the grand atrium of light and air, defining the building as a system of interior cubes linked by ramps and stairways in various directions. New communications systems were installed to connect the foyer and the offices with the upper floors. In the basement studios this same opening offers optimal acoustical insulation. The internal structure is developed through this interplay of presence and absence, of mass, air and light, linked by communications systems of the most advanced technological languages.

The platform over the reception area and the offices offers direct access to the communal service areas. In addition, there is a suspended bridgelike ramp to the second floor, where the rest of the recording studios are located. On the first floor is the bar-restaurant and the kitchen, which opens onto the atrium and enjoys ample natural light from the glazed archways. Flanking this section are two large rooms for equipment and

maintenance. At the highest level, a slightly inclined wall screens and insulates the area containing the smaller technical studios (C, D and E). A long, narrow corridor connected to the ramp provides access to the recording and sound-mix studios.

The acoustical qualities necessary to the functional programme are achieved through both this interplay of insulating spaces and the use of the most appropriate materials and technological systems. The thick reinforced concrete of the new volume protects the neighbouring apartments from any risk from the 24,000 W of sound which may be generated inside. In the various studios layers of beechwood panels on the ceilings not only offer the best possible sound reverberation, but also provide

Plan of the top floor.

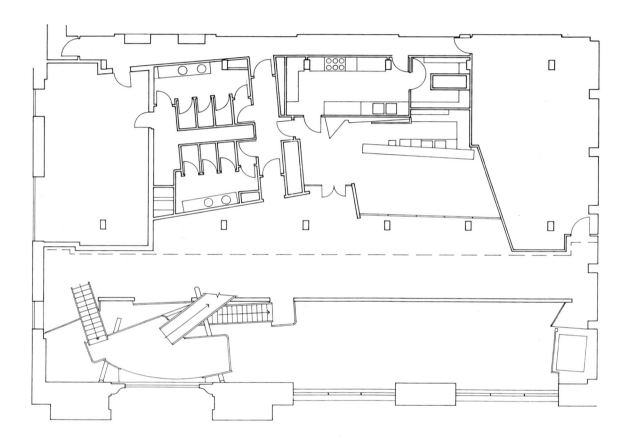

the warm, private atmosphere that is essential to the recording process. The steel doors, the 19-mm thickness of the glass and the soft fabrics help to give an idea of the importance attributed to microdesign. The final result has been acclaimed not only by the media, but by the musicians themselves.

With no prior experience in the field of sound recording studios, the Powell-Tuck, Connor & Orefelt firm has executed a work that completely fulfills the needs of the programme and, at the same time, acts as an instructive model of the synthesis of architecture, design and art. The need to insulate the interior from the adjacent buildings was met by constructing a volume that is independent of the original structure, with a reinforced concrete fabric that acts as a protective screen. The

distribution process is articulated by the grand atrium that dramatizes the interplay of mass and space, and allows light to enter from the exterior. A system of hanging ramps and stairs in true high-tech style offers physical and visual communication and unbroken perspectives. The coexistence of traditional architecture and new techniques, of the coldness and the warmth of the various materials, and of presence and absence lend an exceptional functional and aesthetic validity to this recording studio.

Details of one of the recording rooms.

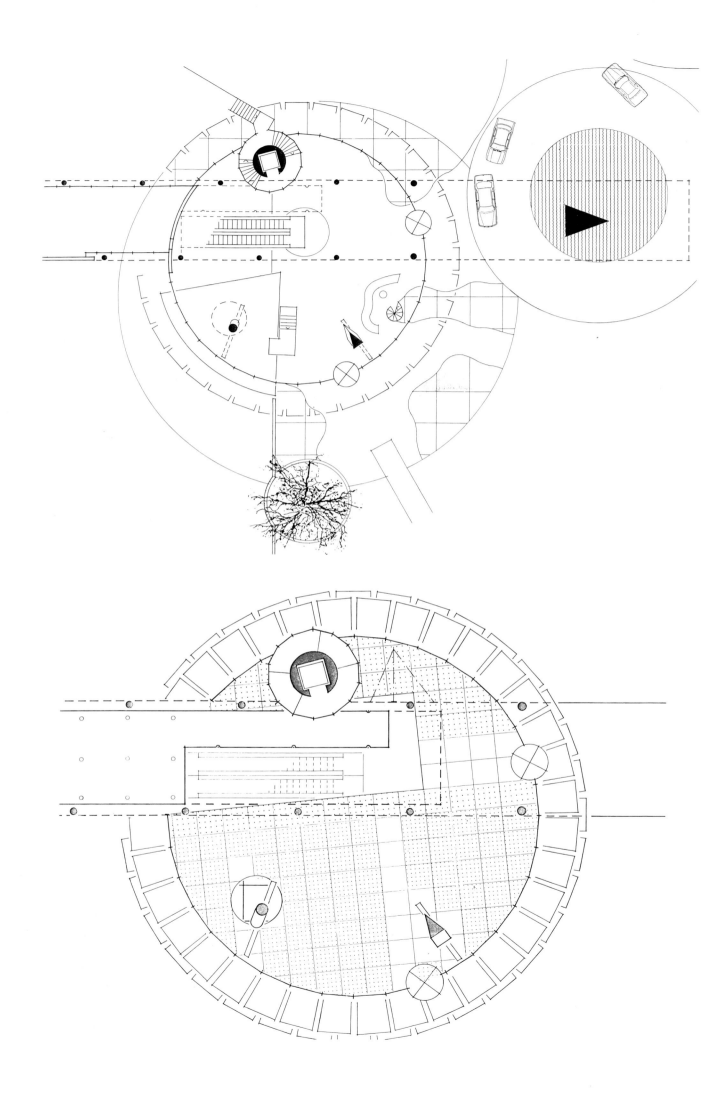

German Postal Museum

Günter Behnisch

In the early eighties, the cultural policy of the Frankfurt Christian Democratic administration began to reap rewards in the form of major new museums and social facilities. Works by Ungers, Bofinger, Meier, Kleihues and Hollein created a new German urban architecture in an attempt to reestablish the city's cultural status in the nation on a par with its growing commercial and financial importance. These structures are arranged along the bank of the River Main, which is now known as "the bank of the museums". To take full advantage of the long perspective defined by the Schaumainkai, the wide promenade that runs parallel to the river, a project was proposed for a museum of the history of the German post office, which was deprived of a suitable site by wartime bombing.

Forty-two entries were presented at the architectural competition sponsored by the city in 1982, and in the end Behnisch was awarded the project. His ingenious solution to the conflicts inherent in the setting was undoubtedly the reason for the selection of his plan. The chief obstacles were of two sorts: the architectural and the topographical. The former concerned the dominant language of the buildings along the Schaumainkai. The river has always been flanked by grand and noble estates that compose an indigenous classical landscape. But their uses have changed in the course of time. Today the villas house insurance companies, associations and, as in this case, museums, so their internal hierarchies have been modified considerably. The exteriors of these historically significant buildings must be preserved in compliance with the official regulations governing monuments. Maintaining the ambience dominated by venerable mansions with their traditional gardens is mandatory. Legislation also protects the trees that enhance the river bank. These plane trees are a decisive factor in the planning of all new construction, so the natural setting has played a key role in the spatial organization of recent buildings.

Regarding the topographical constraints, the project could not expand beyond the limits of the original building, which occupies the best site on the grounds and defines the space available for the new project. Behnisch was left with a long, narrow strip of land and out of respect for the architectural scale, his building

could not exceed three storeys. Its small rectangular site on the west side of the estate is perpendicular to the River Main.

The project was be executed in two distinct stages. The first involved the restoration of the old mansion, by that time in a serious state of deterioration. The process involved a reorganization of the interior to accommodate its new functions. The second stage was the construction of the new building on an uninspiring site, with a physical appearance which would reflect contemporary creative morphology. A stimulating dialogue could be established between the two architectural styles from different periods and expressed in opposing fromal and conceptual languages. Behnisch's contribution was to

Detail of the roof.

The sturdiness of the building's structure is alleviated by the glass walls.

View from the inner courtyard, where classical and modern forms come together.

Cross section.

General plan.

Section of the western side of the building.

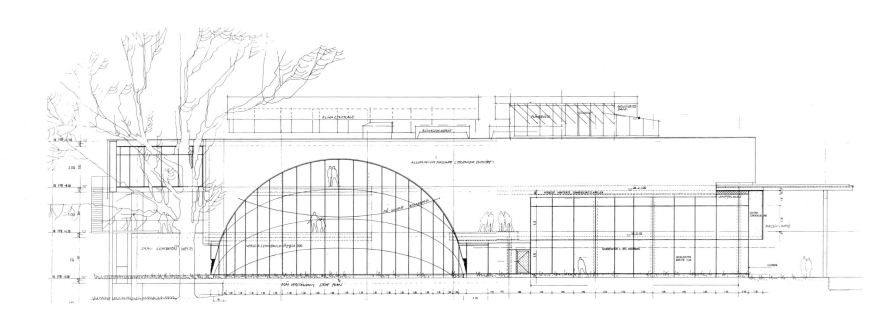

embody modernity, not as an a priori condition, but as an image acquired through the resolution of the conflicts that arose in the course of the planning process.

The new museum had to be parallel to the existing structure and its length was limited by the garden area behind it. The mansion had been built during the Gründerzeit, a period of rampant speculation in the 1870's. From the standpoint of workmanship, the poor quality of the materials did not satisfy the new standards. As far as possible, the original elements and techinques were used, but with an improvement in their quality. Several exteriors could not be rebuilt because no plans or photographs of their original design had survived. The main facade on the Schaumainkai is developed with modern resources and strategies that allude to the new

structure and to functionality. The colour scheme and lighting of the entrance links the two buildings stylistically.

The original internal hierarchy was respected, but it was also adapted to its new function. The mansion has three distinct levels. The ground floor contains a large reference library and a covered gallery in the rear which leads to the garden. The administrative offices are on the first floor, while the second floor is given over to restoration workshops, the photographic laboratory and other support services. The functional programme is distributed between the two structures, thus avoiding a centralization of work in a single space.

To raise the new building, a number of specific obstacles had to be overcome: the dearth of land and the limitations posed by the need to respect the scale and

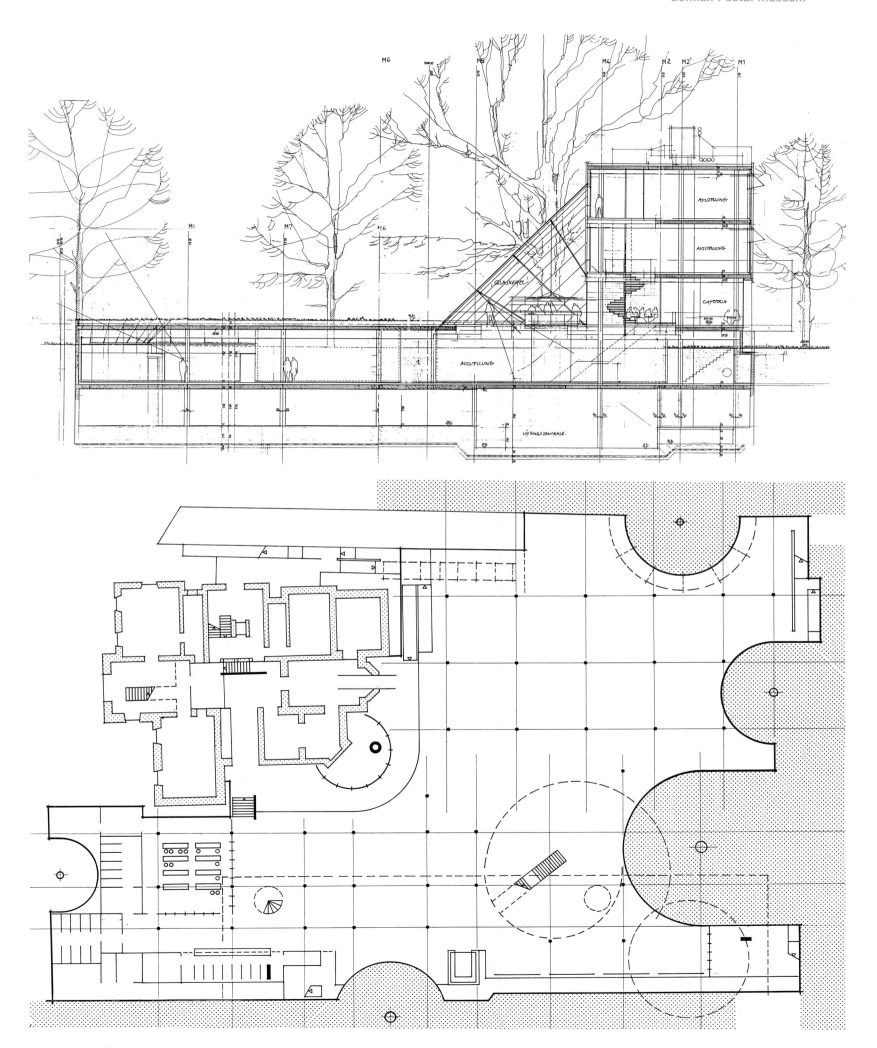

the external environment. As the volume was to be inscribed within a long, narrow strip, the most effective solution was a three-storey, rectangular volume. However, it was impossible to introduce the exhibition programme of the museum into such a small area, so the architect turned to a construction strategy that would increase its spatial capacity. The definitive project incorporates underground levels to accommodate most of the exhibition surface. On these levels a vast area was created which occupies almost all of the land of the estate and includes a large classroom and a portion of the storage space. In this way the rear garden was preserved. The roots of the old trees were left intact by adopting curvilinear shapes that did not impinge on the natural landscape. These are expressed on the exterior as semi-circular, inclined panes of glass, which enable light to penetrate the deepest area. A second underground level houses the technical installations, the garage and more storage space.

The new structure is distinguished by the use of modern materials and techniques, creating a dynamic, elegant image, which is at the same time strong and compact, modelled on the purest Scandinavian traditions. The museum is reached from street level by a short flight of steps leading to a platform. The portico on the main facade has a round skylight and is supported by simple metal columns. Here, some of the curved elements that govern the overall aspect of the new building appear. The

Detail of the glass apse.

The panes of glass are arranged to form fish-tail shapes.

Pure lines intersect to create a harmonious continuum.

The structure allows light to pour in.

contrast between curve and straight line transmits a singular feeling of mobility and free-flowing space.

This fluidity is accentuated through the use of light, flexible materials. The precision of glass and metal allow a composition that best fulfills the purposes of the proposal. The curvilinear forms are vast sheets of high-quality laminated aluminium, used for the first time in these proportions. The use of glass overcomes interior architectural problems by transferring these spatial solutions to the exterior. In the rear garden a conical glass base rises from the ground to join the main volume. The glazing in the entrance combines with the side view of the cylinder to create a luminous visual link between the museum and its exterior sequences.

In addition to the two underground floors, the building develops a vertical scheme that forms three new floors. The strategy of twinning the rounded volume of the cylinder and the rectangle brings together the perspectives and levels on one ideal plane: exhibition. With this new glass roofing the museum takes on a transparent, luminous quality of remarkable elegance. The communication system among the levels including those underground, is located in this most attractive section of the interior. The different orientations and structures of the staircases form the dynamic design of this distributing nucleus, which provides access to the various functional spaces.

On the ground floor is the foyer, the information centre and a circular enclosure in the rear that serves as a projection room. The first floor accommodates the galleries for temporary exhibitions and the curved room

Details of the interior of the building.

directly below opens onto a spacious terrace. There are more exhibition areas on the top floor and its segment of the main facade is a flat, glazed surface. The attic contains a radio transmitter and ventilation equipment. The crowning of the building with the stylized antenna, a reference to technology that lends the construction an overall image of modernity, accentuates the contrast of architectural languages present in the final project.

Behnisch had to overcome very specific architectural and urban constraints, in addition to respecting the surrounding landscape. Each of the obstacles has been negotiated through appropriate solutions, based on a morphology that combines the rigidity of the pure geometric line with the undulation of the curves. Special use was made of these curves in the underground levels

as an elegant method of avoiding the roots of the old trees in the rear garden. The glass cylinder is embedded in the volume to provide light and transparency, as well as to unite the hierarchy of the museum levels on the same ideal plane. The material treatment of the facades and rooms employs modern techniques, thereby generating a dialogue of contrasts with the original mansion. Distributing the museum programme between the two buildings allows the creation of exhibition spaces appropriate to the contemplation and enjoyment of the items on display. Frankfurt has triumphed once more in the realm of cultural promotion through this museum, which combines pragmatism and aesthetics, tradition and the avant-garde.

The combined use of different materials conveys a sense of wholeness in this respect.

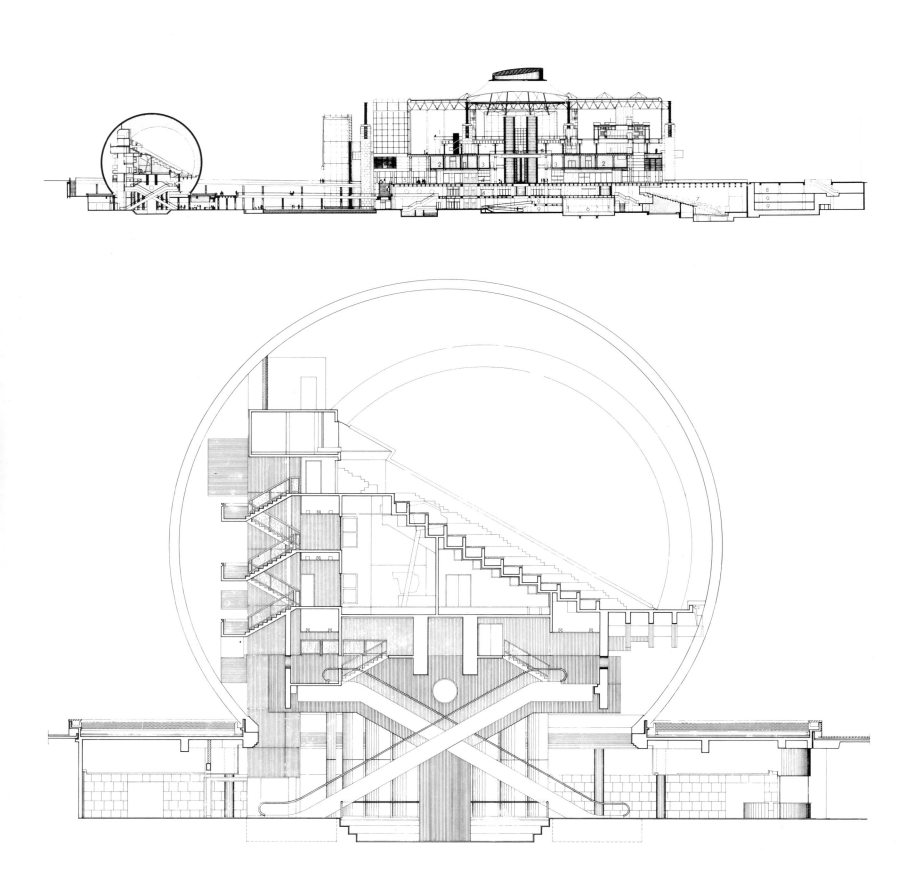

La Géode

Adrien Fainsilber

In 1979, the French authorities decided to carry out an ambitious urban renewal project aimed at radically transforming the area previously occupied by the La Villette slaughterhouses. The plan was to convert the site using some of the existing buildings into one of the biggest and most important scientific museums in the world. The new museum was to be called La Cité des Sciences et de l'Industrie.

A year later a competition was held to choose the best project for the scheme, and one which would embody the dynamic and communicative character which the authorities wished to give this cultural centre. The French architect and planner Adrien Fainsilber was the winner of this competition. Born in 1932, Adrien Fainsilber graduated from the École Nationale Supérieur

des Beaux Arts in 1960. He completed his training in the Royal Academy of Architecture in Copenhagen and the Sasaki Agency in Massachusetts. Throughout his career Fainsilber has combined his work as a creative architect with his work as a teacher. In the late sixties he taught at the University of Urban Planning in Paris. He was in charge of curriculum at the Institut d'Aménagement et d'Urbanisme de la Région Parisienne, director of the SDAU in the Vallée de Montmorency and the Plaine de Villetaneuse. He was appointed architect-consultant to the Ministère de l'Équipement et Logement and l'Établissement Publique pour l'Aménagement de la Défense. Since 1985, he has been a member of the Académie d'Architecture.

Among his many works are the Pôle Central de la

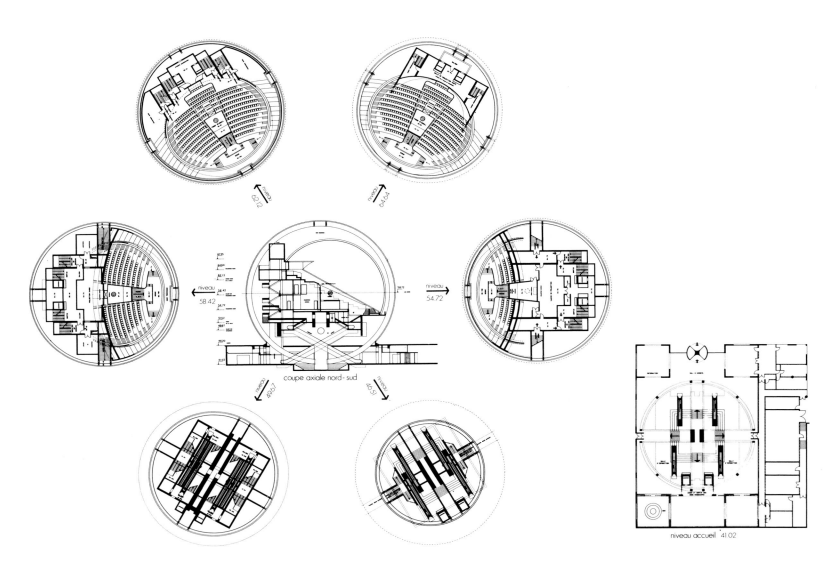

Plan of the different levels inside La Géode.

Elevation of the east and north facades of La Géode and the main museum building.

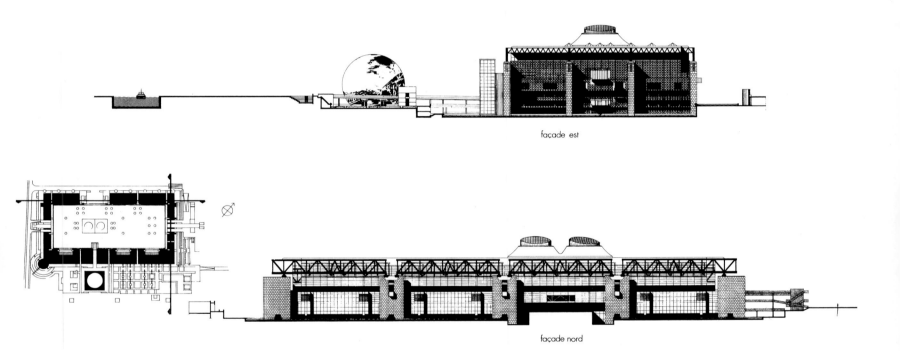

façade est

façade nord

Université Technologique de Compiègne, the Centre *EDF/GDF de Île de France Ouest, the Evry hospital, and the planning of the centre of the* ville nouvelle *(new town) of l'Île d'Abeu. In 1986, one year after the inauguration of the museum, he was awarded the Prix National d'Architecture for his work on La Cité des Sciences et de l'Industrie.*

The whole museum is designed to surprise the visitor who, upon entering this space, penetrates into an unknown world where the latest applications of technological and scientific advances are revealed. But the magic of this museum begins outside as the architecture of the buildings which house the collection is perfectly in tune with the futuristic character which predominates inside. Without a doubt one of the main

attractions of the complex is La Géode, a gigantic steel sphere. This synthesis of a building and a monument houses an impressive cinema where spectacular images are projected continuously to seduce the spectator.

Taking maximum advantage of the expressive force of architecture, Fainsilber opted for a totally innovative formal and structural solution, which represents a complete break with all the traditional architectural canons and fascinates everyone who sees it. Situated in front of the large, glazed, southern facade, in line with the entrance to the reception hall of the museum, La Géode has become one of the emblematic landmarks of La Cité des Sciences et de l'Industrie.

The external appearance of La Géode, which resembles a gigantic glass ball, is tinged with a certain

La Géode appears to float on a platform of water.

intentional ambiguity that contributes to the building's capacity to surprise. La Géode imposes its circular geometry with great expressive force, contrasting clearly with the rectilinear profile of the main museum building. This linear alternation of different geometries has become one of the principal characteristics of the morphology of the museum complex.

With no openings in the skin of the building to interrupt its visual coherence, La Géode jealously conceals the activity which takes place inside. From the outside, the observer sees only a compact ball of steel that appears to float on a platform of water. This composition and the hermetic design of the structure maintains the mystery of the entrance to the building until the last moment. Finally, the visitor discovers that the

entrance is by way of escalators which come up from below the water platform from an area which also gives access to the other main museum building as both interiors are connected underground. The substitution of this totally camouflaged entrance for a traditional one contributes to the air of mystery which surrounds this work by Fainsilber.

But the apparent simplicity of the cinema's geodesic design is the result of a complex, dual configuration in which two totally independent structures make up the internal skeleton of the work. One of them is a branching structure of reinforced concrete composed of a single, central pier extended by cantilevered arms, which in turn support transverse beams. The central pier supports the entire load of the structure of the geodesic dome. The load-bearing structure supports a maximum weight of 6,000 tons and is not visible from the outside. The second component is the covering structure, a geodesic dome composed of 1,500 triangles covered by a steel skin which gives the sphere its mirror-like quality. The geodesic casing is composed of over 2,500 steel tubes 10 cm in diameter in 34 different lengths. These are connected together by 835 Saturne couplings to form a skeletal structure of triangles which supports the 6,433 tetrahedrons of La Géode's stainless steel shell. These tetrahedrons measure 1.2 m on each side and cover the whole exterior, creating the fantastic appearance of La Géode which constantly reflects the sky.

This external casing rests directly on two parallel porticos which in turn rest on the load-bearing piers which transfer the loads to the ground through the solid wall of pre-cast pillars that forms the foundations of the building. The construction of all the load-bearing elements below the water level directly influences the final aesthetic of the building despite the fact that they are not visible from outside. La Géode appears to float on the pond, a device more typical of a work of art than a functional building of this kind.

Once inside the building, the show begins and the combination of images and sound literally envelops the spectator. One of the hemispheres into which the interior is divided is occupied by the tiered seating of the cinema. There are 357 prefabricated seats (six for the

The immensity of La Géode contributes to its expressive audacity.

Side view showing the alternating geometrical lines that define the external appearance of the museum.

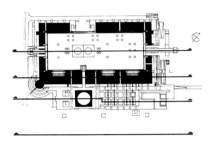

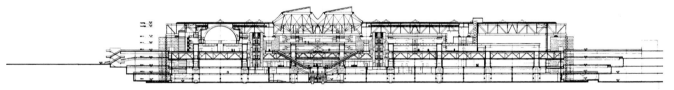

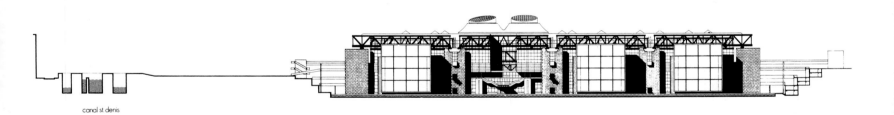

canal st denis

handicapped) laid out on a 30° slope which ensures a good view of the gigantic screen occupying the opposing hemisphere. The placement of the seating in the centre of the sphere permits the screen to surround the audience immersing the viewers in spectacular images.

With a width of 26 meters and a total surface area of 1,000 square meters, this screen is the largest of its kind in the world. These incredible dimensions, together with the obligatory adaptation to the circular geometry of the container, make it possible to increase the field of vision considerably, thereby giving the spectator the illusion of being inside the projected image.

The material treatment of this giant screen had to conform to the specific demands of its unusual size and shape, a far cry from those of conventional cinema screens. The most noticeable feature is the use of perforated sheets of aluminium covered with PVC to eliminate any deformations which might be produced by the curvature.

La Géode is equipped with the most sophisticated, audiovisual technology available today, guaranteeing the best in imagery and sound. There is a complete cinematographic system composed of a laser projection system, diverse cinema projectors, and a battery of slide projectors equipped with mirrors which make it possible to reflect the images off the cupola of the hall. There are other more powerful projectors used to give greater expressive force to the special effects which frequently appear in the films shown here. All the mechanisms responsible for achieving optimum acoustic conditions in

Detail of the stairs which link the different
levels inside La Géode.

Side view of the escalators which transport
visitors up to the cinema.

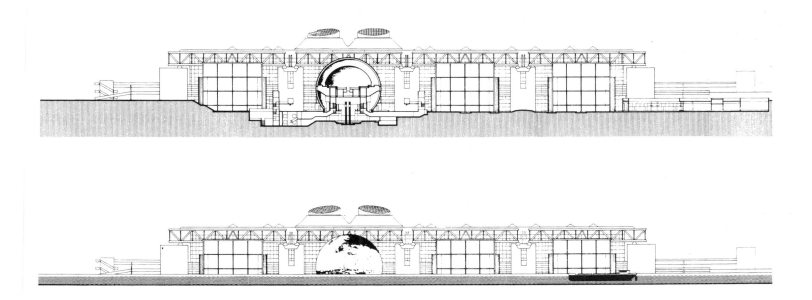

all parts of the room have been positioned in the space between the screen and the cupola. Due to the application of the most recent technological advances in audiovisual engineering, La Géode has become a dream machine where the borders between reality and imagination are blurred, and the spectator is transported to the heart of the most varied scenes.

It can be safely said that the work of Adrien Fainsilber has successfully combined in a single space the most recent advances in engineering and surprising formal audacity creating an alluring attraction which conquers the hearts of the thousands of visitors who come to the museum every year. Once again, science has been put at the service of imagination, and the result is the constant transformation of reality played out by both the interior and the exterior of La Géode. The interior offers the technological advances of the seventh art responsible for fusing fiction and reality, and the exterior – the mirrored sphere – reflects the natural elements, becoming an allegory of the continuous change experienced by the world and science.

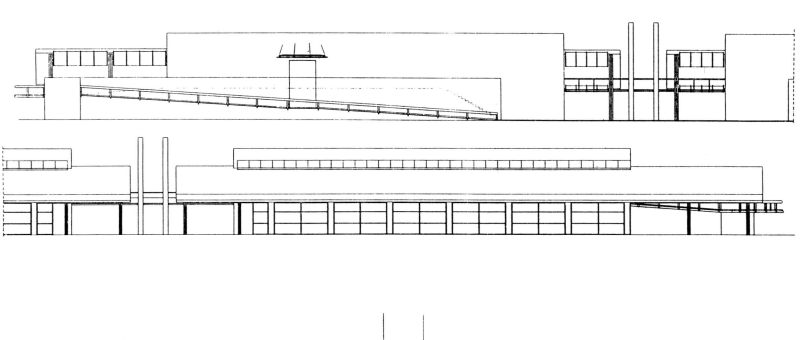

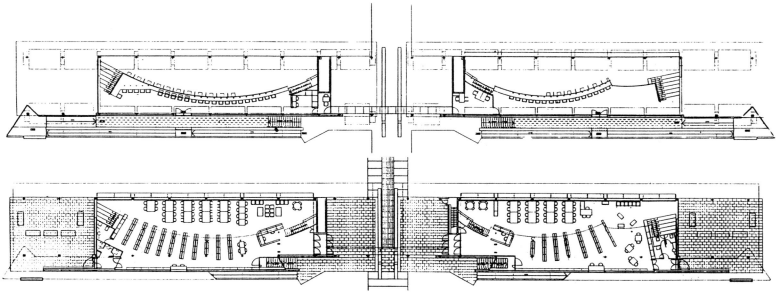

Lateral and frontal cross sections.

Plans of the two floors.

The Joan Miró Library

Beth Galí, Màrius Quintana, Antoni Solanas

The building project of the Joan Miró Library forms part of a larger plan, added as the colophon to a long process that started in 1982 with the construction of the park that surrounds it. It acted as the symbolic predecessor to the urban reconstruction of Barcelona during the eighties.

The library, created by the architects firm of Beth Galí, Màrius Quintana and Antoni Solanas, is strategically situated at the extreme eastern end of the Joan Miró Park, on the edge of both the Eixample and the old district of Hostafrancs. Two aspects appear to act as the departure point for the creative process: the deliberate search for light and silence as fundamental bases to achieving the purpose of the building and its construction.

The work had to fit in with the natural surroundings of the park and within the urban environment of the city itself. The library is in one of the clearings of the pine wood that stretches across the valley and encroaches upon the edges of carrer Vilamarí. In the other direction, the vegetation skirts the curve of the lake encircling the building, coming to an end opposite carrer Consell de Cent. From here there is a view of the natural stone walls that make up the main facade of the building.

It is clear that one of the principal objectives was to blend the work in with its environment and to exploit the natural setting to the full. The most obvious example of this is the lake which surrounds the library, illustrating the need for isolation, peace and quiet that a building of this nature requires. The ranks of cypress trees bordering the

Vertical section of the structure.

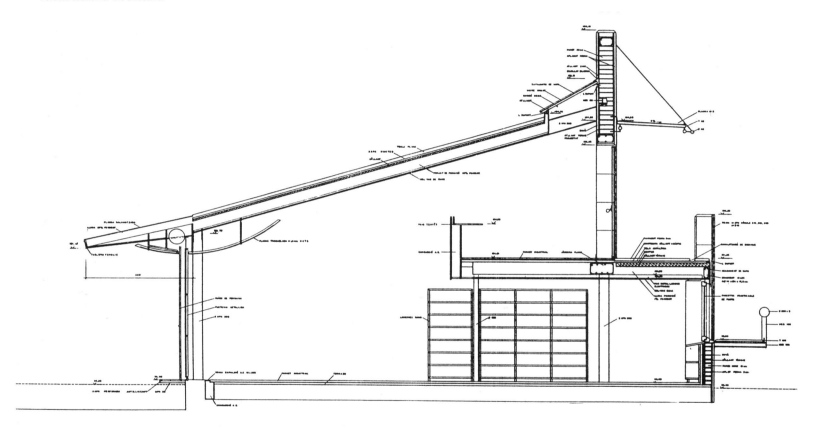

lake are an imitation and natural extension of the stone walls and serve the same purpose. In this way the architectural features and natural elements have been combined to suggest the functional duty of the building from a particular aesthetic standpoint.

The facades of the building have been dealt with in the same fashion. The blank north-facing walls, showing no openings whatsoever, emphasise the character and image of the library itself. This places it within the tradition of the great public buildings of the nineteenth and early twentieth centuries, such as the libraries in Stockholm by Gunnar Asplund, and Saint Geneviève in Paris, or the projects by Boullée for the Roi and Nationale libraries in the same city. The enigmatic walls also evoke the image of book-lined walls within.

Luminescence becomes an essential factor; it is crucial to the aim of the project. The walls facing the park open onto it in search of this element. Sliding glass doors have therefore been used, so that the reading tables leaning against them capture the sunlight in the strategically best way possible from the sloping roof above.

The main entrance to the park, leading from one of the streets of the Eixample, divides the building into two symmetrical parts, one section for adults and the other for children. They are separated by a narrow corridor made up of two parallel walls opening onto the park. These walls act as white screens that reflect sunrays to light up the two entrance porches to the buildings.

This becomes the intersection at which the two opposite circulation routes meet between the main

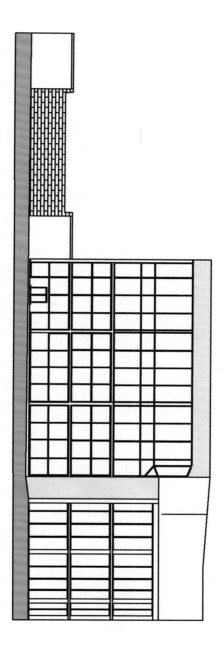

ELEVATION (CANAL SIDE)

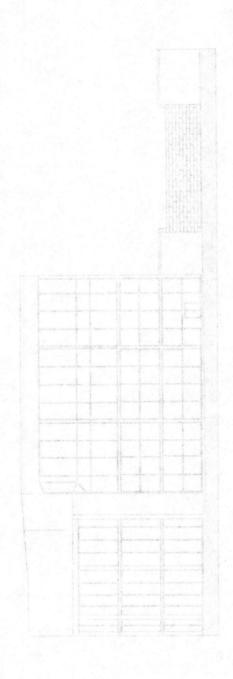

building of the library and the entrance that connects the park with the city. The two wings of the building relate to each other on two levels: through the lobbies by way of parallel walls, and the other through a glass corridor that connects the upper floors of both sections. Apart from this, there is access to the park over a small wooden bridge to avoid a small topographical deformation.

The architecture inside the building is structured around the symmetry imposed by the access route to the park. The base of the building maintains rectangular geometry, while the upper floor is curved. The simplicity of the interior plan is only broken by the slightly complex bare, sloping ceiling, made of stamped plates placed one over the other. The furnishings are functional and austere,

suiting the characteristics of a library where natural light is exploited reducing the importance of artificial lighting, which is allocated a specific task.

At the far end of each block the roof extends outwards creating open spaces for reading outdoors. It is constructed of galvanised metal plate and follows the slope dictated by the bare ceiling.

From an architectural point of view one can appreciate the way in which the creative syntax attempts to mould itself to the encounter between the demands of nature and city life. It is interesting to note how the library project is etched within the all-encompassing concept of creating a place for art, culture and entertainment. The architectural languages rests on unique and individual

The library, and detail of the main entrance.

Marble and metal used in combination on the exterior.

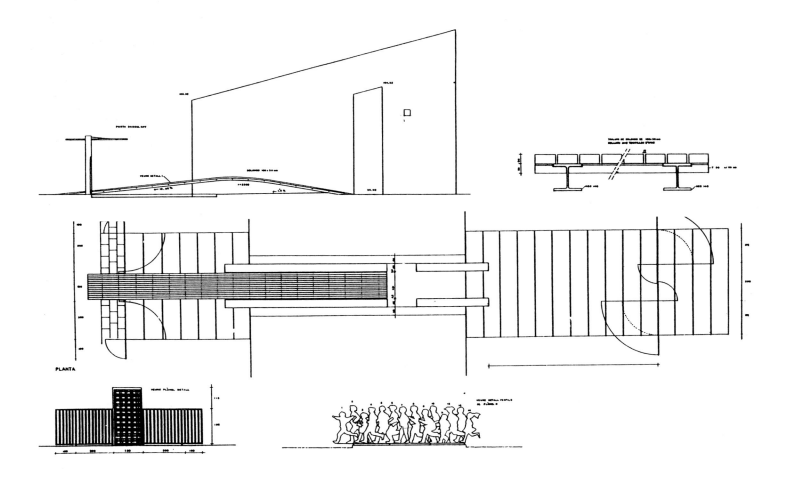

The side ramp leads the visitor to the terrace and the upper floor alongside the stairs, thus providing access for the general public without exception.

features from other disciplines that enrich this idea. This is exemplified clearly through the bronze sculptures by Joan Miró, erected in the covered spaces described above that are designed for reading outdoors. These works, Personnage Gothique, Personnage, Conque, Tête de Femme and Monument, are all definitive of the Miró spirit embodied in the park, which the architects have tried to mirror in the building itself.

Reaching out to the branches of the art world is not limited to the works of the great artist. Other pieces interpret small scenes frequently giving the architecture its own argument for other disciplines. The raised paved path at the entrance to the park with the metal figurines representing children running to the library, symbolises the fusion in various languages of an almost explicit message.

The facilities also have a number of features that relate to theatrical tradition: the bare ceiling, lined with chicken wire, gives an ephemeral, fragile air reminiscent of certain aspects of the world of the stage; the same is true of the parallel walls leading to the park that have such a fiercely confrontational stance, and the rails of ceiling lights so reminiscent of theatrical spotlights. All constitute obvious examples of the intercommunication between the arts, in this case subject to the architecture.

The Joan Miró Library is part of a larger project, the motivation behind a defined initial planning approach. Governed by the demands of both an artistic and cultural environment within natural and urban surroundings, the simple and elegantly designed building stands out but does not evade its function within the cultural agenda.

The library is build over the water, providing a sense of strength. The façade is plain and sturdy.

The metal canopies lend a slightly Mediterranean flavour.

View from the gate.

Access ramp leading to the library.

Detail of a water jet.

The interior affords an interplay of warm colours, parquet flooring and glass walls, the latter providing ample light.

Looking down from the top floor.

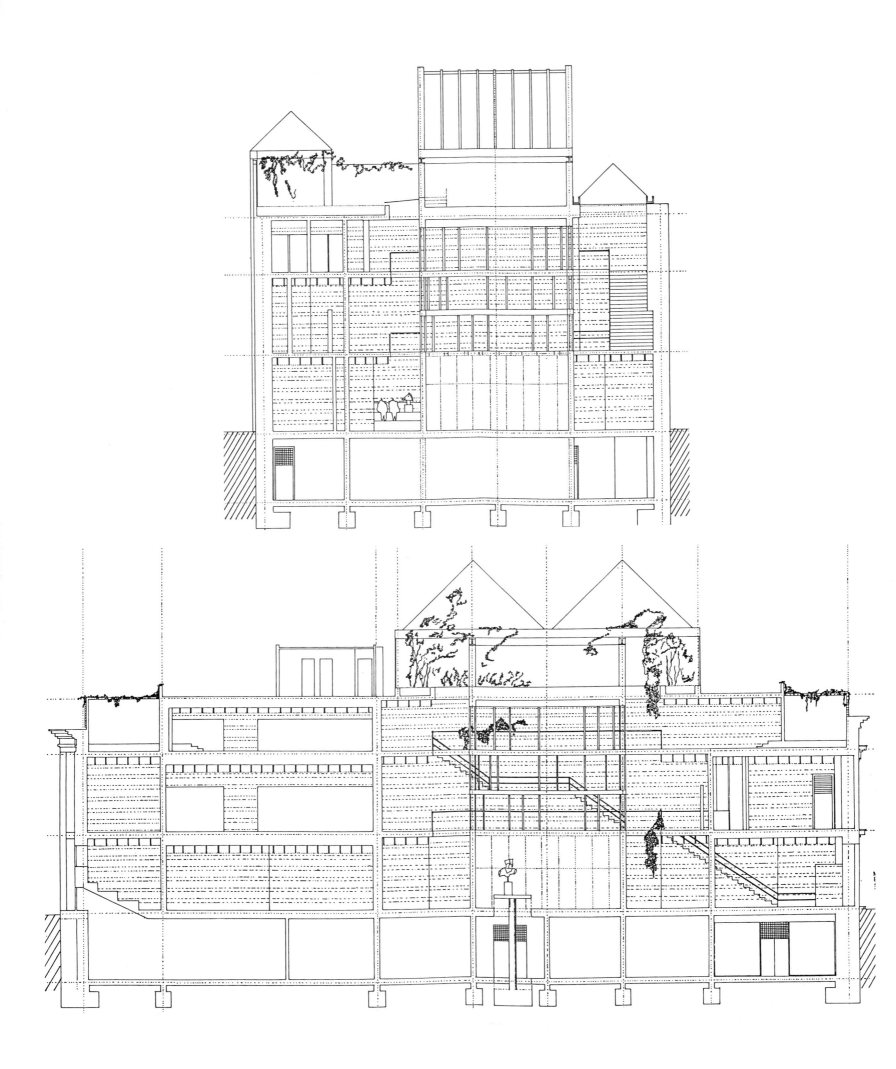

110

Atlantic Centre of Modern Art

Francisco Javier Sáenz de Oíza

The project for a centre for the promotion and exhibition of modern art was a formidable challenge for Sáenz de Oíza. The architect opted for a spare, light, transparent language so that the building would serve as a neutral setting, with the works of art playing the leading role. However, his design, based on simple structures, somewhat indistinct levels, and a subtle search for natural lighting, is an innovative aspect of the building and rivals the art on exhibit. Housing the museum in an existing eighteenth-century structure called for a type of remodelling that would not distort its cultural significance in the city.

The original building is located in the historic centre of the island city of Las Palmas in the old Vegueta quarter. It is exceptionally well-positioned in relation to the

cathedral and the sea, with which both a physical and conceptual link must be established. The stylistic and chronological dialogue between the disparate architectures is one of the basic principles of the process. The renovation task, as a legacy common to all cultures, must have meaning in future ages, offering an understanding of the process of converting a private residence into a museum of modern art.

Seen from the outside, the original two-storey structure is a simple rectangular volume. The eighteenth-century main facade was retained as a thematic element embodying the history of the old city. The first stage of the restoration work involved three of the facades: the scraping and refacing of the walls, which were given a lighter chromatic treatment, the cleaning of all the stone

111

The bar and its terrace are covered over with a glass structure providing both light and warmth.

Ground plan.

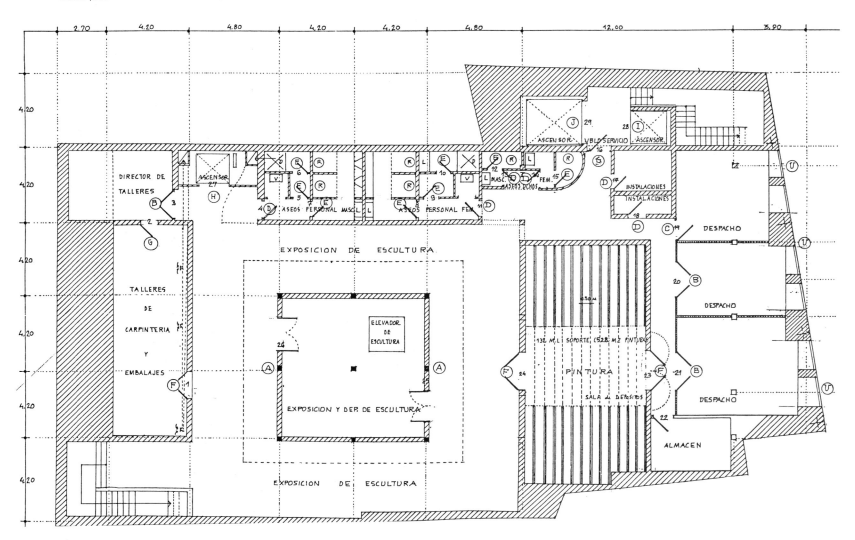

elements, replacing malformed pieces with the same natural stone, and finally the complete replacement of the carpentry with woodwork of the same design in pine. In this manner, the references to the past interact in a striking contrast with the new language of modern architecture.

The interior was gutted and redesigned according to two basic criteria. The first was the need to introduce a new functional scheme which signified a break with the organizing principle of the former residence. To achieve this, the old hierarchical order of levels was abandoned and a new order established which responds to the present use of the building. The second criterion concerns the approach to the problem of lighting distribution throughout the spaces of the museum. The

rooms had been grouped around a central courtyard, the only interior source of natural light. The architect rejected this antiquated composition and used a strategic technique to distribute the light evenly throughout the building.

The first problem was solved by a radically different treatment of the vertical communications in order to build a new structure with no differences in spatial composition. All the levels of the building refer to a single ideal plan: that of exhibition. The distribution of the levels seems to have been designed in hazy outline, with no strict criteria for division, and the inevitable organisation of the layout by heights has been transformed into a unitary space which acts as a focus whose role is to avoid distracting attention from the exhibits.

The conflict inherent in the diffusion of natural brightness and light called for the elimination of the interior courtyard as the only source, The light had to be distributed throughout the levels in proper proportion. To achieve this, the former nucleus of the house was turned into a central opening in the floors of the storeys above, with a structure of columns and crossbeams on the two upper floors that leaves the spatial continuity intact. Light enters from the roof and, with no obstacles to block its path, subtly spreads throughout the almost sculptural layout of the intermediate structure. Through this system, a linear configuration of the old courtyard is achieved, with the greatest possible interior vertical perspective: 9 m. The initial proposal featured a closed pavilion in the garden, but this did not provide spatial unity and even lighting for the entire building. It was finally decided to build a 4-m perimeter wall around the central space, leaving the upper area open so that the light could glance in from the two levels above.

The functions of the structure are organized around a vertical axis. There are four generous exhibition areas. The half-basement accommodates the workshops, storage space, public toilets, offices and technical installations. In the rectangular centre zone is an exhibition area on which light is cast through an overhead opening covered by a grid. The difference in levels between the ground floor and the street is handled by a small flight of steps leading to a spacious foyer, which in

The interior is predominantly white.

Detail of the roof.

Detail of the quadrilateral metal portico, which forms a well-delimited yet open space.

turn provides access to the various functional spaces. The interior precinct is closed off on this floor by a perimeter wall of darker marble and the area around it is reminiscent of an English courtyard. Beyond the obstacle formed by the enclosure, the visitor is led through a series of passageways to a large all-purpose hall. A variety of functions and exhibitions may be held there, and it is provided with projection equipment and simultaneous interpretation services. A small library at one side containing books, catalogues, and prints completes this floor.

The two upper storeys are defined by the form of the central space, which solves the lighting problems and allows the exhibits to be seen from numerous perspectives. The wall below, which closes the central

courtyard, supports white metal structures of columns and crossbeams. The simple construction of this nucleus is remarkably efficient technically. The relative distance between these components lends the volume a notably handsome sculptured effect and suggests an atmosphere dominated by transparency and spaciousness. The various exhibition rooms and their support services are grouped around this core. The area closest to the main facade houses the archives, and in this way an over-explicit dialogue between the two architectural languages is avoided. The space occupied by the old library contains a meeting room and a large storeroom for new artwork.

A staircase located on one side of the building connects the floors. It is built against a partition wall and, starting in the foyer, it rises through all the floors of the

Plan of the first floor.

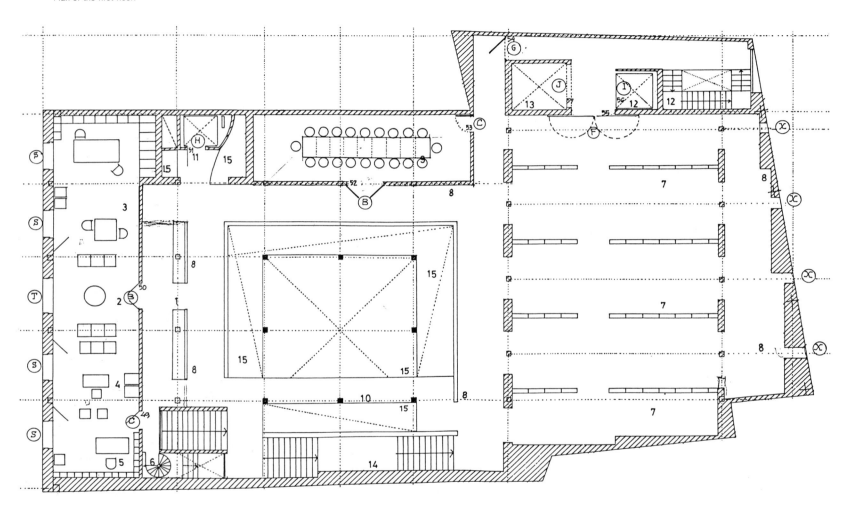

interior facade, terminating on the top floor in a new metal scale that leads to the terrace. The main section of the staircase is made of concrete blocks faced with fine stucco, and the steps continue the flooring of finely textured white marble. The white-painted steel of the railings is repeated in the metal passageways that cross the English courtyard. A hydraulic elevator system completes the physical circulation pattern of the whole.

The other remarkable architectural aspect of the building is the terrace. The panelled ceiling of the open space and tubular columns support a lounge. Soft light enters through the sides of the roof and is evenly diffused throughout the interior. This restaurant/greenhouse crowns the building and its glass walls offer the finest views of the old Vegueta quarter, the cathedral and the sea. The terrace stands out among the rooftops, with its angular enclosure of white wooden lattices, so typical of the island. The centre of the room is protected from direct sunlight by pastel awnings. Several problems are solved by this procedure: first, the museum can be found amid the confusion of domestic rooftops from the perspective of the sea; and second, a dialogue of styles is established which contrasts the various architectural forms.

Sáenz de Oíza's project for the Atlantic Centre of Modern Art seems at first sight to be a simple labour of restoration. The main facade of the eigteenth century residence retains its original splendour, and from the street it is impossible to imagine the unique process of transformation of an antiquated interior which could not

The interior is characterised by the sturdiness of its walls and the use of marble.

respond to the new functional programme. The problems of the hierarchical order and the lighting were solved through a simple and ingenious strategy; the positioning of a central structure of widely spaced crossbeams and columns in the form of a metal cage that acts as the internal distributor. This system manages to suggest a great transparency of the dividing lines that refer to an ideal plane – that of exhibition – and to distribute the light evenly throughout the floors. The crowning of the building is an innovation that clarifies the new structure and gives perspective to the whole. The use of materials with elegant textures and finishes and the soft, delicate colours of all of the elements help strengthen the image of brightness and light in a building designed solely for the most complete enjoyment of art.

Details of the interior. Light metal structures provide a harmonious contrast to the flooring and the facing on the walls.

Plan of the second floor.

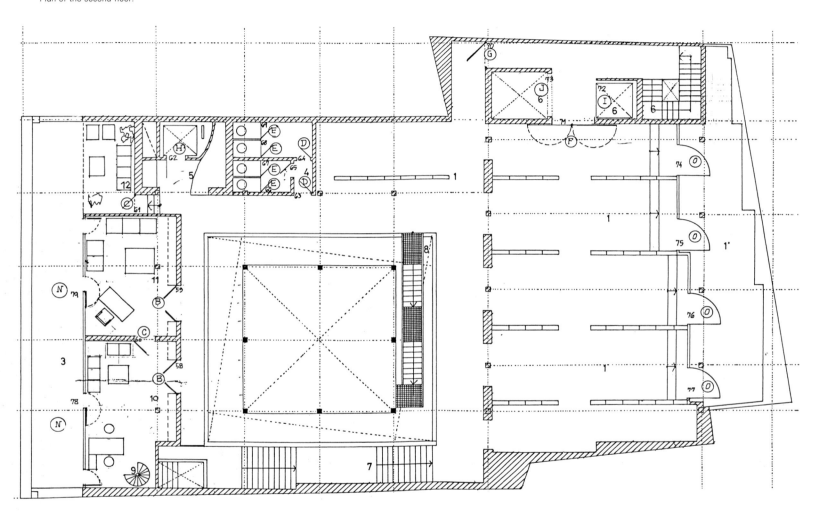

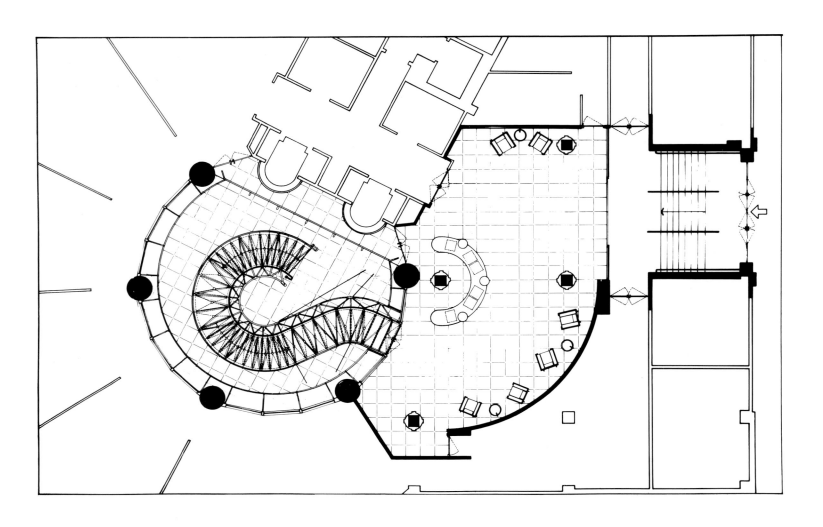

Plan of the building.

Jardine House

Eva Jiricna and Michael Hopkins

In the autumm of 1989 the Eva Jiricna firm was invited by Michael Hopkins & Partners to participate in the design of certain sections of Crusader House (later renamed Jardine House). This was a recently constructed eight-storey office block in London's business district that housed the Jardine Insurance company. The commission consisted of lending certain areas of the interior an impressive corporate image, dramatizing the distinctive identity of the insurance company. Thus, the intervention was confined to the most significant public areas. The first of these is the entrance and the reception area on the level of the street called Crutched Friars. The second is the central atrium with a stairway that leads down to the lower floor containing the four executive dining rooms. Finally, on the top floor of the building, a conference room was to be planned, which would include a technical device to provide protection from direct sunlight.

The existing volumetric characteristics influenced the interior design process. The structure is articulated around a highly vertical cylindrical space, surrounded by curved interior partition walls that are ordered by five large circular columns. This overall pattern, based on curved lines, is partially echoed in the reception area, the radial distribution of the offices and, most prominently, on the top floor, which is roofed by a huge glazed dome. Thus, Jiricna and Hopkins had to adapt their design to the controlling geometry of the building: the curve.

The major difficulties confronting the architects were structural. For example, situating the dining rooms around the central atrium called for a modification of the original

The circular design of the staircase and the
building as a whole gives the house a light,
ascending note.

Detail of one of the meeting rooms, topped
with a dome.

Elegant colours and materials were used in
the design of the interiors.

layout of the building. The central opening had to be
lowered several meters in order to introduce the dining
rooms in the basement of the building. This procedure
resulted in a difference in heights between the main foyer
and the dining room level, which was solved by one of the
most spectacular elements in the intervention: the grand
staircase.

But before taking up the development of this
communication system, the entrance and reception area
will be considered. The entrance from Crutched Friars
opens onto a stairway that terminates in a transitional area
whose laterals provide access to the various wings of the
building. Directly ahead is the spacious foyer, with its
irregular morphology combining curves and straight lines.
The predomination of the curvilinear is emphasized by the

treatment of the elements and of the furniture. To the left
the space becomes more curved. The transition is
established by the reception desk, designed by the Eva
Jiricna firm, and its semicircular structure is centred
around one of the five cylindrical columns.

The articulating axis of the area of intervention is the
core space of the interior courtyard. Its circular form and
its sunken floor required an effective solution to the spatial
morphology and to the problems of physical
communication. The excessive vertical tendency of the
eight floors of the building called for visual attenuation to
lend expressive unity to the whole. To achieve this, the
planners designed a sumptuous element with futurist
references. The freestanding grand staircase, which has
become a trademark of the Eva Jiricna firm, spans the

Large windows bathe the interiors in light.

Detail of the base of the staircase, built in metal structures.

difference in levels created by the lowering of the central atrium floor. At the same time, it resolves the conflicts stemming from the cylindrical form of this space, which distributes all the functional areas of the building.

This stairway descends from the reception level in a wide, gentle slope. Its forms turn inward naturally, adapted to the curvature of the lateral partition walls. The impression of weightlessness is reinforced by its independence. With no supports from the floor, it is sustained only by tension wires to the walls, whose glossy, bright surfaces multiply its reflections throughout the interior. Stainless steel was used for the structure and the black granite of the flooring is repeated in the steps. The stairway is a precise, elegant answer to the needs of the space, transforming a simple physical connection into an exciting, attractive process.

In this project by Jiricna and Hopkins, it is possible to appreciate the way architecture and design work together to define a corporate image for the client company. In this case, the project was confined to the more public spaces of the reception area, the central atrium and the conference room on the top floor, but within these limited domains, the planners have successfully created several identifying symbols for the insurance company. The predomination of curved line, the distribution and communication solutions, the uniformity of the materials, and the interrelationship of the functional areas were the basic goals of the intervention. The architects have successfully achieved a stylistic execution of sober elegance, a synthesis of advanced technology and a sensitive interpretation of spatial problems.

View of the glass dome.

Metal and glass interplay constantly throughout the building.

The fittings display at the same time suppleness and rigidity of form.

All the features of Jardine House come together to create the effect of transparency and light.

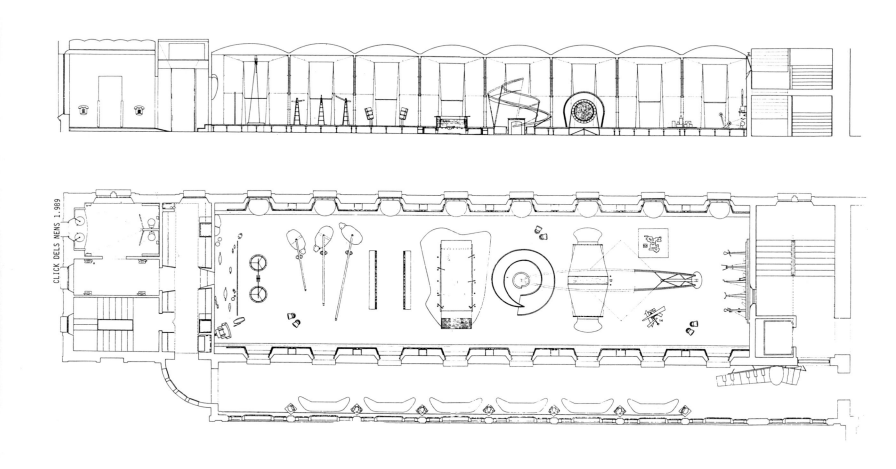

CLICK DELS NENS 1.989

128

Click dels Nens

Alfredo Arribas, Miguel Morte and Javier Mariscal

The Click dels Nens occupies part of the ground floor of the Science Museum in Barcelona. The project is situated, in the general layout of the building, next to the main entrance and a gigantic pendulum in the foyer. The space it takes up is similar in composition to the other floors in this modernist building. It has two readily distinguishable areas: a long corridor that faces onto a patio at the back of the museum which the intervention has restored to its original appearance and secondly, the rectangular room which houses the science exhibition.

The corridor distributes the space and is an ideal place for parents and others to watch the activities going on in the main room. It has a functional purpose in dividing active and passive participants. The inner wall of the facade that looks onto the patio stands in contrast and forms a separation between the child's world and the adult's world.

Next to the corridor is a large rectangular room measuring 8 x 27 m which originally had eight doors giving onto the passageway laid out in a symmetrical line, with eight windows opposite and a vaulted ceiling. The main room has a few smaller rooms leading off at the back to the cloakroom and washrooms, designed to be used by accompanied children.

The various rooms are connected in the form of an itinerary. The eight doors from the room have been closed off and now the corridor for parents and other adults connects only with the auxiliary facilities. These are located in a long small space at the end leading to the cloakroom and washrooms through a small passageway

Pure, simple lines form a unified whole.

Detail of the toilets.

where the giant telephones are situated. This passageway narrows and becomes the only entrance to the main room. Only the children and monitors to guide their activities are allowed to pass through the tall narrow gap forming the entrance. The floor is at a higher level so there are two staircases leading up.

The old building has been transformed into an apt place for its new functional uses. The idea was to make a false interior room which would fit inside the original structure without affecting or damaging it. The walls are covered in aluminium plaques and glassed-in rectangular shapes that shield the lighting and the air-conditioning system. The floor has been raised to 40 cm above the original ground level so that cable installations to supply the various models could be laid underneath. The

elevated level also reduced the size of the doors to a height of 1.40 m thereby converting them into simple viewing holes so that adults can watch the children as they explore the show. It also helped to reduce the room to a scale more suitable for children.

The majority of items are not fixed to the general structure of the building. They are put around the room standing free and away from the walls so that they can be individually substituted without disturbing the general organization. In a formal sense they are positioned separately, although conceptually all the models are placed according to an initial itinerary.

The relationship, between the various models or components and the content they imply, arises as the result of a two-fold proposal. The journey through the

The play and learning areas are demarcated by means of semicircular railings. The interior is decorated in neutral tones and metallic sheens.

Detail of one of the play facilities.

The play facilities display an extremely modern design set off with pastel colours.

basic scientific principles was developed from suggestions from teachers and scientists. Theoretical propositions arise from similar previous experiences that in some way affect the formulation of concepts which can then be applied to the new proposal. The greater freedom in creativity is a result of the planning of the designers. Getting to the content must have a purpose that is educational and fun. It is teaching that is far removed from traditional rigid and unbending methods, it is teaching transformed into a source of amusement and participation.

The original aims of the intervention were based on two complementary levels: the conceptual level, assessed by experts, which lies in the content, and the aesthetic level, created by the designers, through which the

theoretical proposals are established, using colour, form and any other valid feature. They attempted to achieve a balance between science and fun and this is the basic principle behind the nature of the exhibition. The balance rests in this case on a project designed for children who receive stimuli which they think of as play, but which are in fact the first step towards contact with the world of science. Play, experience, investigation are simple words that lose their conventional meanings in a child's world.

The first of these two levels is centred on the search for an order which fulfills the theoretical guide lines and the conceptual content of each component, while giving priority to the original concept. The exhibition also had to be credible and clear, and this was another requirement the designers had to bear in mind when the project was

Pure geometric lines blend into one another.

An original chest of drawers.

View across the main area.

A combination of a wide range of materials with educational aims.

Blue light bulb with metal arms.

The colours interplay and contrast.

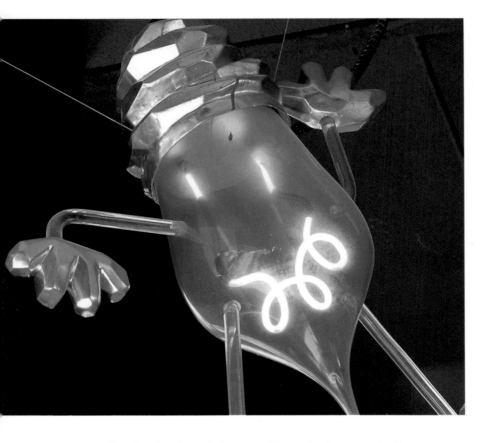

on the drawing board. The most important groups, in the sense of content, were concepts involving body, substance, earth, movement, and comunication. Teachers and scientists established an itinerary calculated to make the children respond to the different stimuli offered by the arrangement of models.

From the second point of view, that of the designers, several factors are particularly noteworthy. Firstly, the fragmentation that this kind of exhibition often suffers from is avoided. Usually, the models are broken up into small groups with too many explicit messages and overall comprehension becomes muddled as a result. In order not to fall into this trap they opted for a unitary structure. The whole exhibition is condensed into one room with sufficient space to house the models. Communication

between child and work is helped by the use of large sculptures, made accessible because they do not represent their purpose or how to use them. The machines are self-explanatory and themselves encourage experiment through their size and position although monitors may also offer guidance or suggestions.

The neutral futuristic environment, the treatment of dimensions, forms and materials, the conceptual itinerary, everything, in fact, is based on making the discovery of scientific knowledge fun by injecting childlike fantasy into a world of science and imagination.

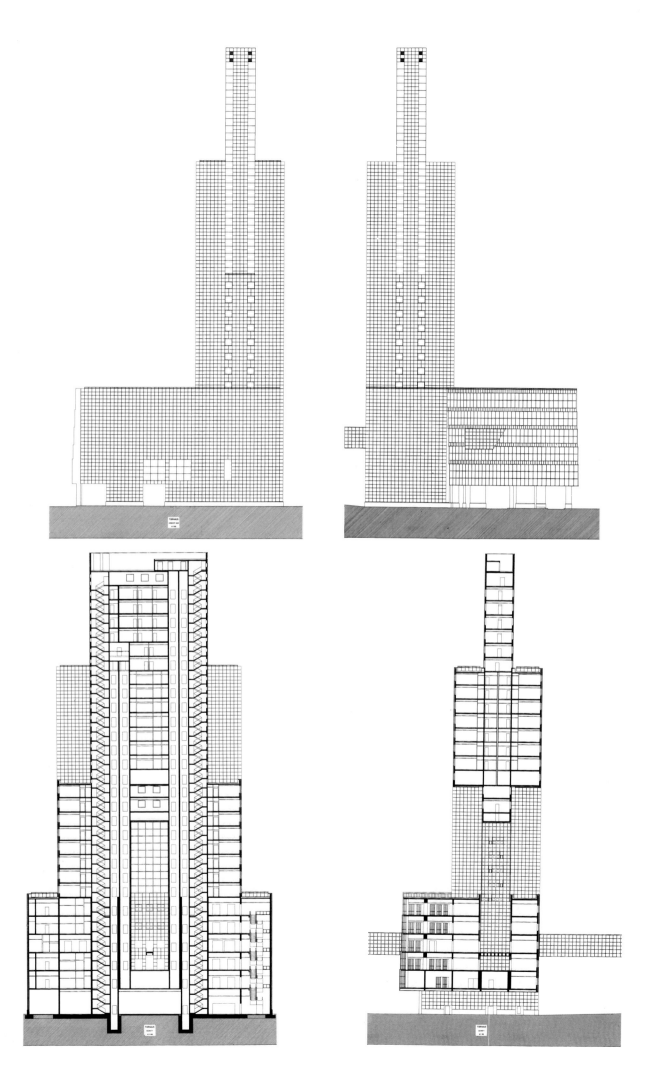

The Torhaus

O. M. Ungers

Frankfurt is politically and economically committed to formidable financial and commercial growth. Through effort and investment it has been assumed that it should be converted into one of the primary European commercial centres and junction of all the roads which run nearest the dissolved iron curtain. The growth policy has resulted in the construction of numerous skyscrapers in the old city, symbols of monetary wealth and richness. In order to add flavour to this power and clothe the enormous amount of business with a more cultural image the city has also launched a large programme for new museums. In this way the material benefits of the skyscrapers balance those which are more spiritual, typical of a culture which has been commercialized at the same time. The Frankfurt Fair, together with its large

banks, is the most representative and active institution related to this new prosperity. It consists of 3 km of pavilions and galleries which have continued to grow behind the unusual Palace of Festivities, a halfway mix between a ship and a coliseum initiated in 1909 by Von Thiersch. Some years ago the fair decided to use renowned architects in the design of large, anonymous premises. Thus, Murphy and Jahn began construction work in the best location; a new suite and large office building at the entrance to the fair from the city centre. The O.M. Ungers office was responsible for the large gallery and a skycraper with offices, which are both described here.

The Torhaus is located in the city centre of Frankfurt, in Germany, in Central Europe near to the access to the

Section of the ground floor.

The Torhaus is composed of an area in which to walk, at the same time allowing moments of rest on the lineal journey which is created by the fair's various pavilions.

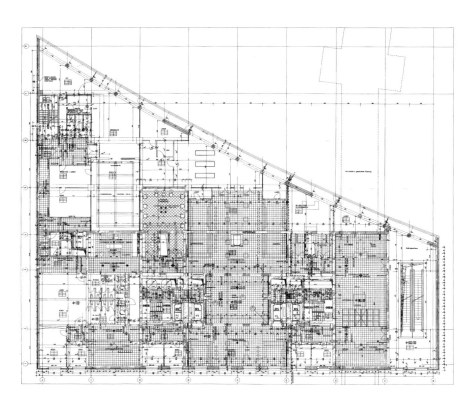

motorway which runs towards the west of the city and which carries a large amount of traffic. Furthermore, two railway lines cross the area on elevated tracks creating an open triangular zone between the lines which earlier hindered the fair's activities. The solution to overcome this obstacle was this attractive but functional building which made access to both parts of the area possible.

O.M. Ungers was born in Kaisersesch, in Eifel, Germany, in December 1926. After attending school in Mayen (1932 and 1947) and doing military service (1945-46) he enrolled at the Technical University of Karlsruhe where he obtained his degree in architecture in 1950 after three years of study. While studying he set up his own architect's study in Cologne, Germany. In 1963 he held the post of professor at the Technical University of

Berlin, Germany, and he obtained the professor's chair for urban design. In 1964 he opened a new office with a branch in Berlin. From that moment his teaching activities became more and more intensive and complete. During the course years of 1965, 1966 and 1967 he was a visiting critic at Cornell University in Ithaca, USA, as well as dean of the Faculty of Architecture and senator of the Technical University in Berlin. The following year he held the post of vice-dean at the same university. Between 1969 and 1975 he was president of the Department of Architecture at Cornell University. From 1970 he was considered as a licensed authorized architect in New York State which allowed him to open another office in Ithaca, USA. Between 1973 and 1978 he worked as a professor at Harvard University, and between 1974 and

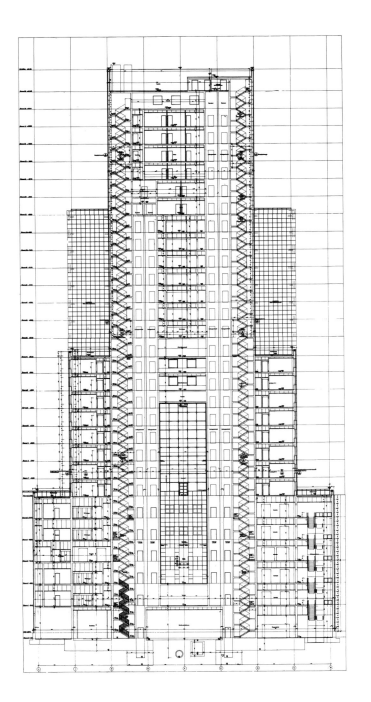

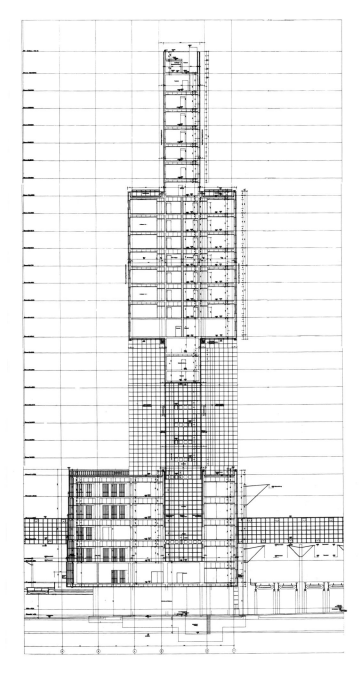

Longitudinal section of the work plan for the Torhaus.

General view of the Torhaus with its horizontal crystalline foundation and the skyscraper rising up.

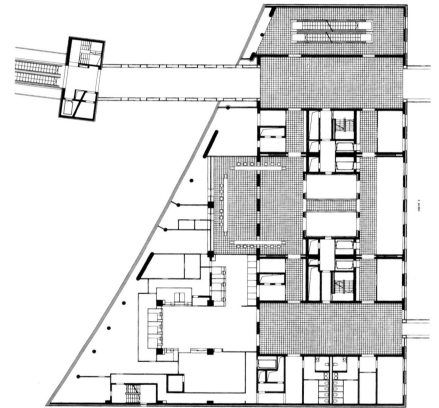

1975 as professor of architecture at the University of California in Los Angeles, USA. In 1975 he was also nominated as faculty professor of Cornell University in Ithaca. In parallel, his work as an architect continued developing with great success, with the result that he opened another office in 1976, this time with a branch in Frankfurt, Germany. Three years later he began work as professor for the High School for Angewandte Kunst in Vienna, Austria (1979-1980). In 1983 he opened his last office in Karlsruhe where he received his basic education. Finally, in 1986 he was nominated as professor of architecture for the Kunstakademie in Düsseldorf, Germany. His worldwide projects allow him to be a member of the San Lucca Academy of Rome, the American Institute of Architects, the Association of

German Architects and the Akademie der Wissenschaft zu Berlin. Among prizes received for his prolific work the Grosser BDA-Prize of Germany (1987) and the Prix Rhénan Strasbourg (1989) are those which stand out.

In the location where the railway sleepers meet in a triangle, which up to a short time ago obstructed the view of the fair's grounds, there is now the building of glass and stone, called the Torhaus. The name refers to its location since it has been specifically constructed near the access to the motorway transforming it into a symbolic entrance to the city of Frankfurt ("Tor" means "door" in German). This characteristic of being an access, of a door confronting the world, allows the fair to open itself up to the outside, to the international market. The Torhaus constitutes the centre of the Frankfurt Fair and

View of the skyscraper consisting of two structures connected to each other: one inner glass building and the outer one of stone which surrounds and protects it.

The openness allows the visitor to understand and verify the actual dimensions and
the morphological rules inherent in the construction.

View of the glass-like roof protecting the *via
mobile*, characterized by its arch shape.

offers optimum conditions for varied use and a large
number of activities.

This piece of architecture produced by O.M. Ungers
offers multiple connections for traffic to the outside such
as an elevated path for pedestrians which connects
directly with the large car parks of pavilion four or a direct
route coming from the Theodor-Heuss-Allee providing an
even faster access. The structure basically consists of a
horizontal foundation and a skyscraper which rises up on
a slightly irregular base which occupies the entire area
between the two railway lines. The most important
service facilities are found in the first unit distributed over
the four floors. The first floor holds the play area to
entertain the youngest children; the second floor holds
the hairdresser's and food stores since it has been

conceived as being the floor which is dedicated to
physical well-being. The third floor has been designated
to consulting services and aims to answer any question
as far as possible or solve any problem. Thus, it holds
information centres, interpreting services and their
offices. Finally, the fourth floor holds businesses and the
press. The southeastern corner houses the heating and
air-conditioning system. A via mobile, that is a path for
pedestrians, destined for the affluence of visitors runs
along the third floor. The foundation ends at a height of
27 m where there is a road surface for traffic. The
skyscraper, appropriately named with its 24 additional
floors rises up above the road. The building thus has a
total of 29 floors and a height of 117m.

The skyscraper consists of two structures connected

to each other: an interior glass building and another of stone on the outside which protects and surrounds it. Behind the impressive facade its 24 floors house the fair's administration offices with its usual openness towards the international world of business. This innovative production offers alternative, multifunctional areas above the roof tops of Frankfurt which may be used in a very different way. The distinct units are divided into areas of 400, 300 and 100 m^2 respectively.

The skyscraper with its ambiguous nature responds to a wide-scale, clear idea modulated by constructive perfection of the object itself. Its appearance offers a precise, strong image of a large door resulting from the union of the two buildings which symbolically indicate the centre of the fair by means of a giant billboard fixed to a large support. Its definite identity comes from its original contribution to the transformation of an architectural typology whose most recent background offers very few significant examples, at least in Europe. This production by O.M. Ungers accepts this challenge and adopts the physiognomy of a door transformed by its enormous size into the evocation of a triumphant arch. This has a connection with the paradoxical situation of the structure inside the fair since it is not located in one of the far ends but in the centre of the complex. Therefore it is not a door which separates an inner area with an outer one, nor does it signal the transition between two zones but serves to connect two places which up to that time were

View of the empty space which is crossed vertically by the lower nine floors of the spectacular house of glass.

separated by their non existence: the east and west end, divided by two railway lines which defined the triangular area in which the fair was developed.

The door structure is thus defined as a nucleus, not so much a geographical one nor as a centre where various paths run from it, but as place where one may take a momentary rest and repose on the lineal journey created by the various pavilions of the fair. Furthermore, it has been constructed as a crossroads which may only be accessed by crossing the bridges which are built over the roads. The Torhaus is two-directional on this obligatory route and therefore enhances both functions.

O.M. Ungers knew that only a new radical shape which could not be confused with other spectacular

buildings erected in the city of Frankfurt could be convincing in this complex. However, within the magnificence caused by the fantastic richness of this production the selection and the use of materials or the design of the details which appear on it eliminate everything which could err in the immediate perception of thematic clarity of the piece. The neutrality of the square grate, the continuity of the raw materials present in the facades or the apparent absence of any mediation between the project stage and the construction phase constitute the various aspects which strengthen the sculptural aspect of the object and explain its apparently unrestrained size. In fact, its enormous dimensions were necessary in order to relate the building to the world of

View of the *via mobile* which is situated in the centre of the grounds and runs directly through the Torhaus or service centre.

View of the inside of the *via mobile* which comfortably distributes the visitors to all of the fair's pavilions protecting them from bad weather.

In its interior the use of materials as well as the design of the details avoids detracting from the thematic clarity of the structure.

fantasy through the use of analogies, even running the risk of causing a feeling of discomfort, a direct consequence of its excessive, definite and constructive purity.

In the glass house the openness of its lower floors is what stands out. With its nine floors this space, which is found to be exclusively filled with passages, is converted into an illusionary and fantastic place as well as into an area characterized by vertigo; with the sides covered by mirrors reaching the ceiling and on moving around inside they even transmit a feeling of being privileged. Standing here the visitor may understand and verify the dimensions and rules inherent in the construction, precisely by perceiving the height and depth existing between one element and the next. With this nucleus O.M. Ungers emphasizes that for

him architecture is an object of attraction.

The Torhaus at the Frankfurt Fair is a daring selection which does not grant superficial and ephemeral concessions to those with whom commercial architecture is indulgent and for those for whom simple publicity tricks are used. On the contrary, the structure summarizes contemporary idealism which, by referring to something sublime with regard to classic aesthetics, assumes an ideal tension, an exaltation, dynamism and, with respect to the visitor, a willingness to be elevated spiritually. It is in this way that the aesthetic, austere, cold, rational and abstract kingdom of O.M. Ungers is finally accessed. The fact that the world is still capable of arousing attraction today constitutes perhaps the most optimistic lesson which may be learnt from this spectacular skyscraper.

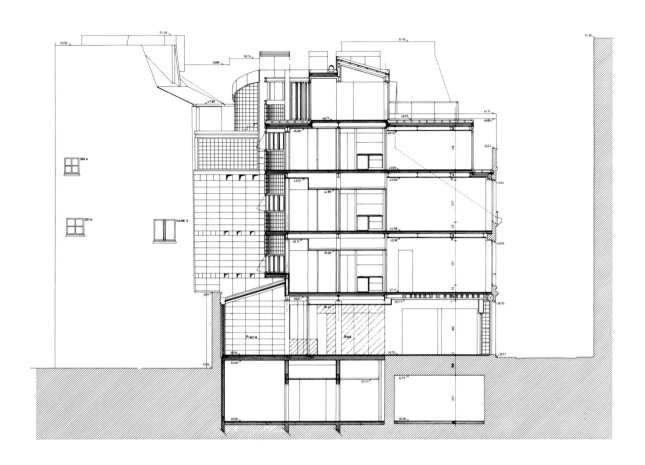

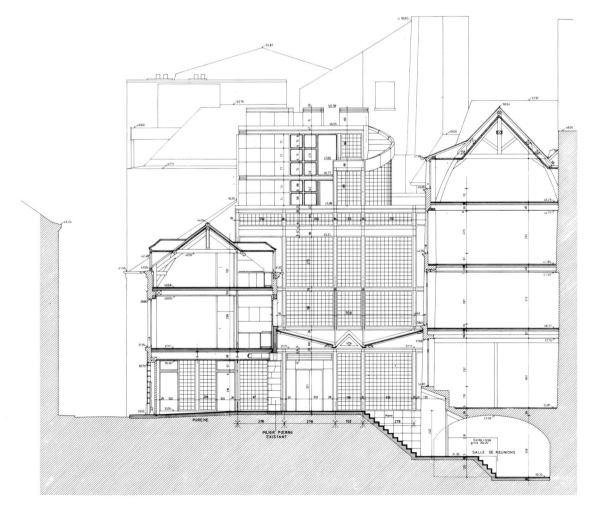

148

Maison Suger

Antoine Grumbach

To the architect Antoine Grumbach, the project for this human sciences building represented considerably more than a mere conversion or renovation of old structures. It is a genuinely creative intervention in which the new and old exist side by side in the same dimension, and historical tradition meets with eclectic innovative strategy. The architect, Antoine Grumbach, has used this synthesis as the starting point for his proposals. He has combined the original structure with new ones in search of a specific objective: to set the scene for transparency, light and clarity in all their forms and aspects. The functional programme for a comfortable living and working environment is perfectly suited by these criteria. The building's urban setting has enabled Grumbach to expound upon the possibilities for architecture in the city.

The ingredients which have gone into making Maison Suger have created an immediately apparent stylistic exercise in contrast and expression.

The idea for the building originally arose in 1985 when it was suggested that a residence with bedrooms and studies should be built for foreign students of human sciences and made available through the rectorates of the Paris universities. The proposition was backed by a number of other institutions, including Volkswagen, which created a foundation to administer the project.

One of the most influential factors in the design of the building was the site chosen for this residential complex. The Rue Suger is a small arterial street located in the sixth arrondissement in Paris, not far from the Fénélon Institute and the Faculty of Medicine. This ancient district,

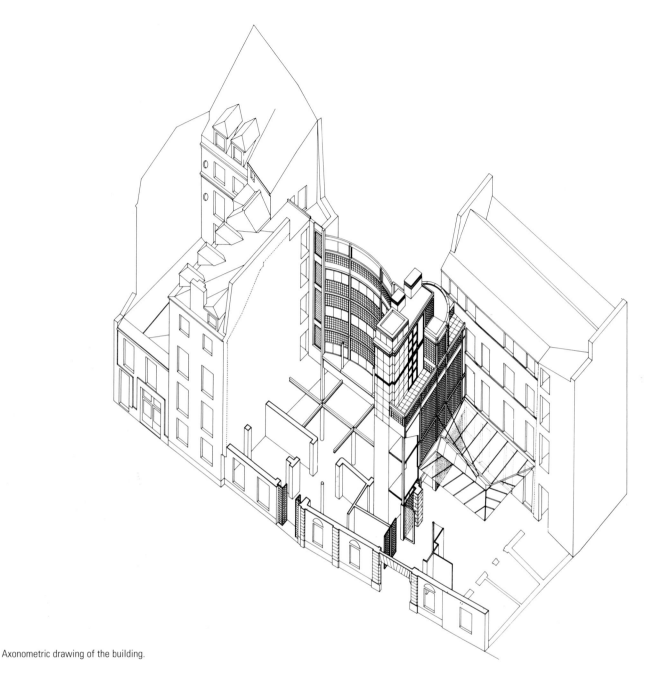

Axonometric drawing of the building.

the Latin Quarter, abounds in features of symbolic and historical importance. It lies between the Seine, Rue Danton, Boulevard Saint-Germain and Rue Dauphine, haunted on both sides by the memory of the Sartre of Rue d'Ulm and Sartre of the Café de Flore. The context of the building was considered ideal for one of such a specific nature as it combined evident cultural connotations and the historical legacy of the city.

The final programme involved the construction of a building that would have 33 residential units, plus an extension to the École Maternelle (a kindergarten) next to it in the street of Saint André des Arts. There old buildings, dating from the seventeenth and eighteenth centuries, formed the initial basis for an innovative intervention which left only the original facades intact in

order to retain their historical character. Any suggestion of it being simply a renovation of old buildings disappears as soon as one looks closely at the construction techniques used, which enabled a dialogue to be established between architectural values and languages from different periods.

The proximity of the school and the state of disrepair of the old supporting structures led to a decision, in the summer of 1986, to demolish them, which would clear the way for the construction of the future building. Nevertheless, the idea of preserving the old structures was thought to be feasible, and so an in-depth study was initiated to investigate the skeletal framework of the buildings and culminated in the granting of permission to build in December of the same year. The first steps involved preserving the facades, renovating the old stone work and moving most of the old walls to lay out the new apartments.

The most important part of the project, however, was not this, but how the original building frameworks could be subsequently articulated and linked. Thus the facades of the old buildings and the renovated interior, together with a startling juxtaposition of materials, shapes and volumes, created an innovative contrast between trends and influences from different periods. The method chosen for this all but impossible endeavour was based on a series of criteria that appeared to be totally contradictory. Spatial unity was considered to be of the utmost importance, but this would have been an

extremely difficult task had there been an attempt to solve each specific problem through a common solution. The heterogeneous structural features were treated in a way that was completely revolutionary, in terms of form as well as concept, and this formed the starting point for the intervention.

The layout of the lodgings was planned according to the original spatial limitations of the old buildings. However, they had to communicate with one another and certain spaces, such as a general entrance and common rooms for studying and social gatherings, were also needed. Methods that were a far cry from any conventional approach were used to effect changes which would create a sense of homogeneity. Grumbach

View of the façade.

Looking up at the interior walls of the building.

Detail of the highly original glass roof, which exploits the contraposition of weights and forces.

Cross section.

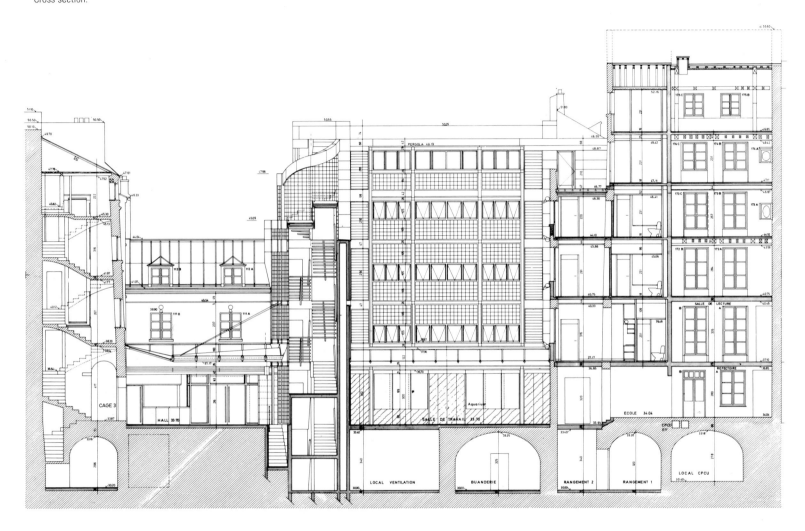

planned the project with one clear aim in view: to attempt a visual transparency that would react in contrast to the opacity and the compact mass of buildings in the old quarter of the city.

In order to exemplify this opposition, the architect opted for demolishing the central structures to put up a new building which would have two interior facades. These caused a visual break in surfaces and spaces but achieved a conceptual unity in light and clarity. A new interior was thereby created to physically connect the distinct atmospheres of the future building. This structure would functionally serve to house the studies, lavatories and staircases.

The exterior of the building is constructed of square metal grid structures set with small clear glass tiles. The

flat facade running perpendicular to Rue Suger has an uncompromisingly geometrical appearance which, combined with the technically innovatory materials used, provides a visual contrast. The only entrance to the building is by way of the courtyard of number 20 of the narrow street, making a spacious reception area fronted by the new facade. At the height of the first floor a glass skylight is suspended over the open patio, held by a framework of steel bars slanting down to a central piece. This structure lets in a vast amount of light to form an ideal foyer.

From here, the glass roof provides a view upwards showing the contrast of materials and forms of the building structure: the old interior facades made up of symmetrically placed windows and sloping roofs, and the

General plan.

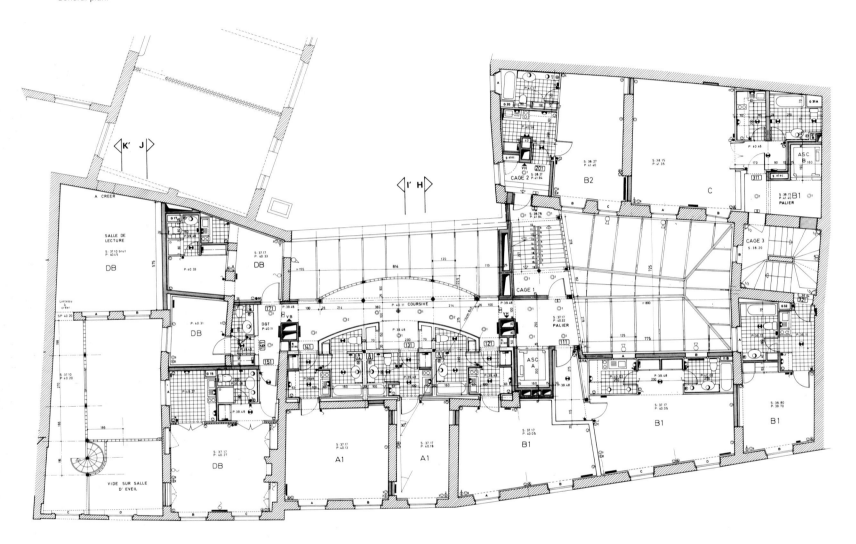

stark metal parts of the other facade. Passages and stairways lead off from the foyer (to administration and meeting rooms on the ground floor, and upstairs to the large common workroom on the first floor). The stairs leading to the upper floors turn into a spiral staircase on the fourth floor, which can be seen protruding as a bow-shape on the exterior. The curve softens the stiff perpendicular lines of the facade and also acts as a visual transition to the new adjacent facade which continues the curving outlines.

This second element runs parallel to Rue Suger, closing off the area inserted where the three buildings converge. The main characteristic of this facade is its emerging curved outline that ends on the top floor in a small open oval balcony. The exterior is in the same metal

grid structure, except that the glass is arranged lengthways to highlight the division into storeys. Direct light, therefore, enters on all floors and there is a view of the whole facade through a skylight, built at first-floor height and supported by a metal frame. The large study on the first floor consequently has a comfortable working atmosphere with lots of light, enhanced by the interior decoration, cosy furniture and artistic contributions by Pierre Buraglio.

The way this module has been constructed shows a spirit of genuine creativity, new functionalism and conceptual unity. The communal areas are located here, stairs and corridors that communicate with the rest of the building and the area where the old, unconnected buildings join. Other rooms, notably the large meeting

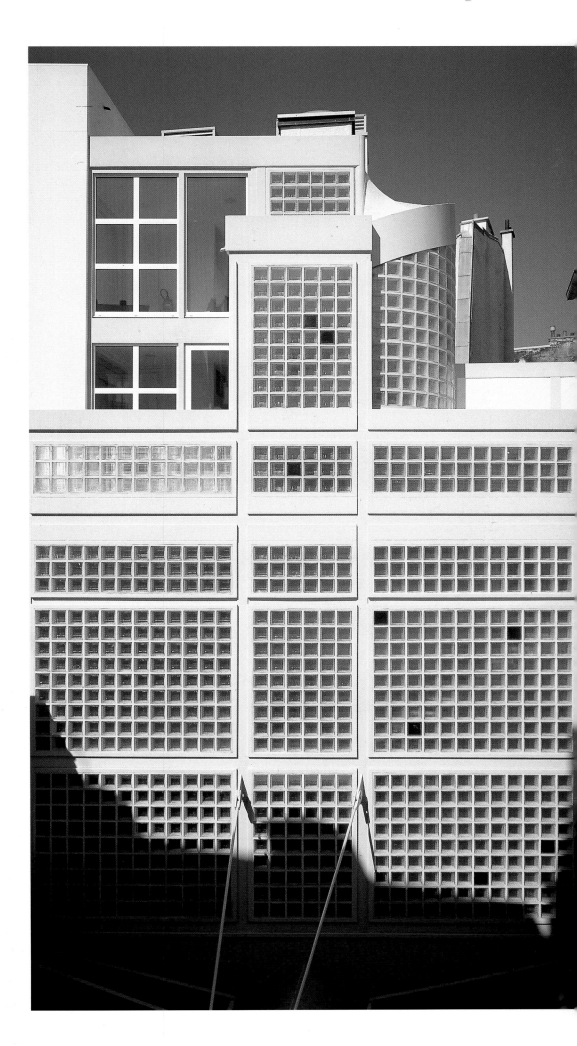

The use of glass as a construction material for the walls lends a warmer, lighter feel to the building.

Details of the interior of the house.

room, are located in the basement. The programme for extending the kindergarten at number 16 was reduced to the construction of an outside courtyard which would not interfere with the old structure. The most important part of the whole project lies in how the old and the new tie together; a glance will take in preserved stone pillars juxtaposed with flexible materials such as metal and glass.

It goes without saying that Grumbach has not limited himself to a job of mere restoration; it is, on the contrary, an example of unique architectural creativity. Any conflict caused by the variety in styles of interior areas has been dealt with in unconventional ways. The architect has opted wholeheartedly for the most innovative procedures, concentrating most particularly on transparency and the

entire span of its possibilities. In fact, this is fundamental to the whole project, having tremendous power to unite the contrast between traditional and modern architectural languages, and it is the key to the artistic merit in this exquisitely accomplished typological exercise.

Various different natural materials are used together: marble, glass and stone.

Parquet flooring adds a feeling of warmth.